BEING
A MAN
IN
A WOMAN'S
WORLD

BEING
A MAN
IN
A WOMAN'S
WORLD

JAMES E. KILGORE

HARVEST HOUSE PUBLISHERS
IRVINE, CALIFORNIA 92714

BEING A MAN IN A WOMAN'S WORLD
Copyright © 1975 Harvest House Publishers
Irvine, California 92707
Library of Congress Catalog Number: 75-37136
ISBN-0-89081-018-4

Printed in the United States of America

DEDICATION

To my father,

who spoke few words but taught volumes.

INTRODUCTION

At lunch some time ago, a friend said, "Someone needs to write a book for men." This is a book for men. It is not *the* book, but it is an attempt to share some of the insights I have found helpful in working with men in my practice of counseling. I deal with men every day. I believe these ideas work for single as well as married men. It is also a book that will help some women gain insight about the men in their lives. There are ideas here that work for fathers, too. They grow out of my relationship to the three teenagers at our house and the families with whom I have worked.

I want to convey the joys as well as the responsibilities of being a man in a woman's world. When a man learns who he is and discovers the pleasures of relating openly to other men and women, his movement through life can be fascinating and exciting. Being a whole man is rewarding and fulfilling. The intent of this book is to aid you, the reader, in your own quest for balance between the responsibilities and the fulfillment in these relationships.

It is *time* for this book. The liberation consciousness has rallied women to a new and forceful identity within or outside the "movement." Some men are threatened and some are stimulated, but none goes unaffected. Books, magazines, television, and radio provide advice for *women* on how to behave in our world, but here are some practical, workable ideas for *men.*

We men need to be aware of ourselves and clear about our direction in this changing world. I'm excited about our future. I think you'll sense this as you read.

My thanks to Don Highlander, my associate, for his constant reminder that I need to take time to write. My wife, my children, and the people who have touched and enriched my life by their trust have contributed to this manuscript in ways they alone may recognize. To all of you, friends and teachers, thank you!

James E. Kilgore
Atlanta, Georgia

FOREWORD

Being a man in today's world is a much more complicated thing than it was in grandfather's day. We men need all the help we can get to understand the complexities of the relationships swirling about us.

Dr. Jim Kilgore, in his new book *Being a Man in a Woman's World*, has given us some of the best new help available to understand our place and purpose in the world. In his warm and conversational way, Dr. Kilgore illustrates what it means to be a healthy and wholesome man.

Not only in relation to our women—wives, mothers, daughters, and friends—but also in relation to other males, especially our sons, Dr. Kilgore helps us to orient ourselves more clearly and confidently. He helps us to understand our ministry, our roles, and our value as men.

C. Ray Fowler, Ph.D.
Executive Director
American Association of Marriage and
Family Counselors, Inc.

CONTENTS

PART 1

BECOMING
A MAN

The man who knows right from wrong
and has good judgment and common sense
is happier than the man
who is immensely rich!
For such wisdom is far more valuable
than precious jewels.
Nothing else compares with it.

—Proverbs 3:13–15, *The Living Bible*

1

IN THE BEGINNING

*You came into my life and loved me and
somehow I became me.*

—Chantal

It was dark. I felt wet but warm. As she moved, I responded to her movements. I stiffened and the movement of my leg seemed to startle her. She reached down and pressed her hand against me. There was a flow of energy between us that sustained me. I needed her. I could not live without her, and yet in a unique way I fulfilled her. We had already developed a relationship that to break off would bring pain. I was alive with curiosity, and my energy at moments strained her capacity to respond.

I was in my mother's womb and would remain there for another four or five months. Then came that fateful day when the buildup of pressure in her body forced me out into the bright, airy world. I no longer was protected by the warm sac in which I had developed.

I didn't know what the world would be like at that moment. The harsh realities began to dawn on me when I had a firm introduction to pain with a forceful application to my posterior. After being scrubbed up and put in some warm wrapping, I experienced the beautiful nurture of being fed at my mother's breast. We were together again!

The way we get introduced to the world of women, first intimately and then detached, leaves us with an insatiable curiosity about them! What makes women so exciting, fulfilling, and, at times, elusive?

Mothers Are Always Women

Males never have the opportunity to be mothers. Being a mother may not supersede being a father, but none of us knows what it is like on the other side of that experience. We only know what it's like to interact with women in our world. In those early years it's predominantly a woman's world to which we are introduced. Think of all the things that women—nurses, mothers, grandmothers, big sisters, "Aunt Sarahs"—do to and for babies! I'm concentrating on the baby boy and his relationship to the world of women. Little practical help has been given to man about how they grow up and learn to survive in a world dominated by females!

Sigmund Freud suggested that in the first two years of life a child considers himself "His Majesty, the Infant"! He doesn't distinguish between his own wishes and those of other people in his world. Later he recognizes that difference! Initially he finds satisfaction through his oral cavity. He brings things into his world via his mouth, occasionally he discovers that some things don't belong there! As he grows he sees himself as part of the total universe.

During the second phase he learns that he can give or withhold what others expect of him. Failure to adjust in this period of life hampers his later growth process. Successful development at this level provides a foundation for learning self-discipline and respect for others. On secure sharing experiences he builds positive relationships for handling the conflicts of his future. Unresolved struggles for personal power affect his concern and sensitivity to others' needs throughout his life.

The discovery of his sexuality marks a new period

in his development. He is not the same as his mother; he is different! His curiosity about the distinctions between male and female has begun. How he handles this knowledge, and his subsequent comfort with the new facts he gains, influences how he survives in her world. He is becoming a man.

We Want a Son First

In my practice of marriage and family counseling I have often heard couples express the sentiment, "I hope we have a boy first." Boys are really quite special. I'm glad I was a boy. I had a younger sister. First children, especially boys, tend to be responsible. Often they seek to please their parents and society.

While on a research project for The International Family Foundation, I traveled to South Korea during 1975. I was impressed by the importance given to the birth of sons there. A family with two sons is considered doubly blessed.

In ancient Israel a "near kinsman" had the responsibility of carrying on the name of the deceased male by impregnating his widow and giving the child the name of her former husband. It was part of the levirate marriage customs.

Other cultures point to the importance of heirs, particularly males, in their society. Boys continue the family name! For many couples it may be that a desire to continue the family is what influences their wish that a male child be born first. In these ways boys are "special."

Becoming a Man

Being born physically a male is only the beginning of that process of becoming a man. There are significant influences that contribute positively or negatively to your sense of masculinity.

Almost every man I have seen in my office can identify a single person who helped shape his early life. Some men are blessed with more than one "significant other." Surprisingly, it may not always be a parent. Someone sees you as "a special little man" and invests time and energy in your development.

If one person in my young life made me feel "special," it was my grandmother. She noticed all the little things that other people overlooked. Though meaningless to others, she called attention to them in a special way that reinforced my growing self-esteem. I feel a certain pain for every young man who has not had loving grandparents who have bestowed upon him that unique kind of favor that only they can give their own grandchildren.

My grandmother was notorious for her "favoritism" in my case. I was "the special grandchild"! I can never forget her love. Her constant reassurance of my worth helped build a base of confidence in myself, without which I would be less than I am as a person. She complimented and praised my initial efforts. She encouraged me in difficult times. She helped me laugh at myself—a gift that led to a sense of humor.

Being a Man

Boys are special to their fathers, brothers, grandfathers, and uncles. They discover models in these men. Older men are guides in the process of self-identification for boys who emulate them. Men bear great responsibilities in teaching (whether deliberately or unknowingly) what it means to be "manly." *All* men teach *some* boys lessons that affect their future. The attitudes shown and the actions displayed powerfully demonstrate the *masculine* patterns. Most important among these is the way men show boys how to relate to women.

A Father's Gift

"The greatest gift a father can give his children is to love their mother." Those words are on a plaque mounted in the reception area of the Northside Counseling Center here in Atlanta. I believe these words are true. Living them out before my three teenagers is a challenge; enjoying them with their mother is pure pleasure.

Mothers Make Deep Imprints

It is the opposite relationship with which I am concerned now. How does the input of women affect the developing male? His mother is most significant. Sister, grandmothers, aunts, and cousins play a part.

I have become convinced by the comments of men in my office that women, particularly mothers, dominate their development. In our society no relationship—including that of fathers to daughters or sons—is as potent as that of mother to son. Someone other than the physical mother may fill this vital spot in your life because of absence or abdication. No one has such natural access to your emotions as does your mother. Her invisible psychological umbilical cord can strangle you in adult years. Her remembered nurture can sustain you long after her body is in the grave.

Mothers begin our adventure in the world of women, but there are more females in our futures. It is appropriate now to consider how their expectations affect us as we grow.

2

GROW UP,
LITTLE MAN!

Love does not dominate; it cultivates.

—Goethe

Few of us can remember what it's like to be a baby. A baby boy gets treated in pretty much the same way as a baby girl. He is cuddled, cooed at, smiled, and "faced" at by all sorts of adults who want to see if he can smile, has teeth, or will cry! As long as he's a baby this is fine, but there comes a point in a boy's life when things change. It's no longer right to be a "little boy"—now he's got to be a "little man." This is a perceptibly harsh change for many developing male egos. Why shouldn't he be able to go on crying when something hurts, or playing with the dolls, or enjoying soft textures, or occasionally wanting to be the mother when he plays "house" in the family or with the neighborhood children? Why should he now always have to be "strong"? Maybe no one knows why, but it becomes a problem which many men struggle with for a lifetime.

One of the common complaints that family counselors hear is that husbands are unemotional, preoccupied, and absorbed in what's going on in their minds or with the pressures of their world. Take Joe, for example—and you know that may not be his real name—who is an engineer. He deals in a world that's precise, a world in which he can always find the "right" answer. No matter what the situation is, he keeps struggling or going back to the drawing board and to the formulas until he *does* discover the appropriate response. He may have chosen to be an engineer simply because he was trained all of his life to control his emotions. To make things come out in precision steps with no unexplained part or loose ends left over is his task.

Work World Versus Woman's World

Rules work well for Joe in his professional career, but when he begins relating to a woman on a one-to-one, intimate basis, he finds himself with no rules, few guidelines, and many frustrations! Inside, he may be asking where all the freedoms have gone. Does his life consist of nothing but responsibilities now? He married "Mary" because she respected him and made him feel important. He enjoyed the feeling of "having all the answers," but her dependence on him for constant stroking and reassurance of his love grows very old for Joe at times. He wants her to learn her own role and function smoothly without expecting and demanding constant emotional reassurance from him.

Mary, for her part, feels disappointed that Joe is withdrawn and distant. She no longer feels able to relate to him. Failing to develop emotional closeness in their marriage, they come for counseling.

"Why are you two here?" I asked. Mary blustered out her story in almost hysterical tones while Joe sat stone-faced and silent. "I'm here because she's driving me crazy with those emotional outbursts! Can you help her?" Before Mary could retort I interceded to describe a diagnostic plan that Joe could "buy."

She had a problem: he was it! The expectations he had attempted to fulfill as he grew up left him few options in manhood. He certainly wasn't what Mary expected in a husband.

Cowboy or Playboy?

Jack Balswick, a noted sociologist from the University of Georgia, said that *men fall basically into two categories: the cowboy and the playboy.* The cowboy is a rather bashful, John Wayne, western-type man who is more at home with his horse than he is with his lady friend. When she seductively bats her eyes at him, all he can reply is, "Aw, shucks, ma'am!" He is more at ease stroking and nuzzling his horse than he is kissing and fondling a woman.

The playboy, on the other hand, is suave, debonair, and casual in his attitude toward women. He is never satisfied with one woman and is always in search of something more—that elusive woman who will end his search! He places no value on any woman in particular and is unable to make a genuine commitment to any one woman. He notices every woman and is intrigued by her uniqueness, and in his own way he needs to find a special place in the life of every woman he knows.

The woman married to the cowboy may console herself in the fact that he doesn't say much, but by the way he acts and the kind of commitment he shows to her, he demonstrates that he does love her. But the woman married to the playboy soon begins to feel used and "passed by" in the parade of younger, more exciting, and more stimulating women.

Joe, the engineer, would have to be called a "cowboy" rather than a playboy. He depended on his actions rather than his words. He wanted logic and not emotion in life and in his wife. Somewhere in the formation of his ideals for manhood a strong implant said "men think—women feel." Unfortunately, Mary's expectation called for a sensitive, compassionate man—much like her own father had been. Their counseling process involved helping them to understand the differences in their own expectations. Then they began to build new goals for their relationship.

What Kind of Man Are You?

If you find yourself uneasy, shy, and reserved, probably you will develop a "cowboy" stance in life. You may engage in heroic feats and enjoy your "silent strength." However, your loneliness in relationships will remain. Very often your "bashfulness" can be a manipulative way of getting attention from women. You may have mastered, knowingly or unwittingly, the art of using your silent strength to turn on the admiration of women. The maternal juices of many women flow strongly toward the shy and introverted man.

The "playboy" type excites a woman's passions. Because he focuses on her, momentarily she feels as though she is the *only* woman in the world. So, the Don Juan is afforded a key to her soul and sometimes to her body. His promise of love completely disarms her—or so it seems. Yet a temporary quality in his devotion undermines the playboy's relationships to her. He can in no way fulfill all his promises, so he fulfills none of them, and he remains lonely.

Resisting Expectations

Every male in the world has to come to grips with the expectations with which he has grown up and how he's going to respond to them. Both husbands and wives resist fulfilling each other's expectations, and this results in constant arguments. Many men make the tragic and sometimes fatal mistake (as far as marriage is concerned) of saying, "I will not meet your expectations." Then they fail to live out their own potential as individuals. In working with numbers of men I have seen the man with great locked-up potential who refuses to be the kind of father his wife wants him to be, and in so doing he often fails to *father* his children! Or in the process of refusing to be the kind of husband she expects him to be, he fails to be a husband at all.

Take the Initiative!

Men have to make choices about the way they fulfill the expectations of the women in their lives. It is an irresponsible cop-out for a man to refuse to meet his wife's expectations and to offer nothing in return. In the maturing process a man must distinguish between another person's expectation of him and his own expectation of himself! In that process he discovers the goals that will guide him to maturity as a man.

A positive thing about the broad socialization process of most boys is that it usually leaves open some kind of initiative. For all the double standards we hold up about sexuality—at least we held them until the Women's Lib Movement hit us in the groin—the man was given the opportunity to take the initiative and the woman was left with the responsibility of containing it. In the past we haven't minded boys doing some "ridiculous" things in their maturing process because "boys will be boys." Every man has in him some "wild oats" that he must sow! In this part of the socialization process is the key that every man can use to unlock the doors of his own potential. Look at the expectations of others, and look at your own qualifications and resources! Begin to develop the kind of "special man" that you really are! Part of the kind of man you become will be indicated by the type of woman you choose.

No matter how big a man he becomes, his desire to relate to a woman in a significant way is going to play a dominant part in his life. Curiosity craves fulfillment not only in his loins and his head but in his heart.

3

UNCHAINED CURIOSITY

*People are lonely
because they build walls instead of bridges.*

I recently saw the Broadway play "The Sponsor" by Ira Lewis, and I was struck by a confrontation between an aging director and an aging actor in the rest home for retired actors. In the play, Phillip, the alcoholic actor, manipulated and cajoled his friend, Arthur, the aging director, into visiting him and reminiscing about old moments of the past. As part of the soliloquy in which Arthur engages as he talks about the past, in anguish he describes his relationship to his ex-wife. He says he has 19-year-old girls waiting to "tumble for him," but he can't get another look from this woman who is twice their age and who, he once thought, loved him with all her heart.

The tragicomedy of that scene, like so many others in modern drama, is that it is so true! From the very first time a man puts his lips to the breast of the woman he calls mother to the last time he touches the body of a woman before he goes to the grave, there is an almost insatiable curiosity in him to know what this other sex is like, a desire to really understand.

We have such interesting descriptions for women—the weaker sex, the fairer sex, or, in marriage, "my better half." And every man is caught in a struggle between the dependence he wants from his woman and the opportunity he seeks to lean on her and draw sustenance from her soul.

The Child Within

The dullest men I know are those who have allowed the child in them to die. They are also the most vulnerable men in relationships to women. As the transactional analysts point out, we have within us various parts, or ego states, which can be identified by the way we function within them. The *parent* is that part of us which is both critical and nurturing, while the *child* is that part of us which is curious, submissive, and rebellious. The *adult* is left with the responsibility of managing the conflict which arises between the two parts.

How quickly man passes on the surface from being a child to being a parent! It reminds me of the poem "When I Was One-and-Twenty," by A. E. Housman.

When I was one-and-twenty
I heard a wise man say,
"Give crowns and pounds and guineas
But not your heart away;
Give pearls away and rubies
But keep your fancy free."
But I was one-and-twenty,
No use to talk to me.

When I was one-and-twenty
I heard him say again,
"The heart out of the bosom
Was never given in vain;
'Tis paid with sighs aplenty

And sold for endless rue."
And I am two-and-twenty,
And oh, 'tis true, 'tis true.

Almost too quickly for most of us the time comes
when we are no longer able to be free, spontaneous,
and curious about our worlds. We appear to be locked
in, bound down by our responsibilities and commitments.

Sometimes in group therapy, when fantasy experiences are provided for men, the "little boy" emerges
again. I'll never forget Bill. He was an executive—
handsome, suave, and extremely controlled. He said
the right words, did the proper things, and acted in
the appropriate manner in almost every situation.
But one night he allowed the little boy in him to fan-
tasize about some experiences of his childhood on the
farm, and it was transforming! His face loosened, his
eyes brightened, and his body relaxed. The most important thing that happened was that he became interested in other people in the group. He became
curious about others. He listened, he asked questions,
and he thought about the answers he got. He again
became a little boy.

That childlike curiosity is a part of what keeps a
man alive. It's part of his anxiety. Soren Kierkegaard
called anxiety "the alarming possibility of being
able." It's part of man's fear and part of his ability to
dream.

True Maturity

The greatest gift an adult woman has given to me as an adult man is the rediscovery of my "inner child." My wife is the "eternal child"—ever fascinated with little accomplishments and always thrilled by the smallest of gifts. Since I am somewhat compulsive, we used to meet head-on. However, her patience and exuberance with life were too contagious! After eighteen years I've decided that it's more fun to *cultivate* the inner child than to *crucify* it. I remember early conflicts in our marriage which resulted in great part from the dominance of the "parent" in me. My life seemed to skip from age 6 to age 26, leaving no time for being a teenager—that transition period in which childishness finds its blend with maturity.

As I struggled with my own maturity in psychotherapy, I discovered a helpful book, *Your Inner Child of the Past*, by W. Hugh Missildine. My own curiosity to know more about the "child" in me has contributed to the maturing process in my life. For many, like me, there is a rapid transition from childhood to manhood. The consequence is the death, or at least a severe restricting, of the inner child. No longer can he be free to "play"; he is a man. He may even admonish himself with the words of Paul, "When I was a child I thought as a child, I behaved like a child. But when I became a man, I put away childish things" (1 Corinthians 13:11). This man, who takes his faith seriously, finds that there is a double bind: the assumed or stated expectations of male maturity, and spiritual depth. Disregarding the Biblical promise and thrust about joy, this Christian can get *deadly* serious about the "maturity."

What is maturity? It is a willingness to assume responsibility for one's own thoughts, feelings, words, and actions. Nothing in that definition forbids joy in one's accomplishments or laughter at one's faults. In many ways it is this "unchained curiosity" that best expresses man's continuing growth—physically, emotionally, and spiritually.

As he flexes his muscles and extends his physical limits, a man's body grows. As he stretches his thought patterns and emotional reach, his mind grows. In the quest for spiritual maturity, his soul grows. Interestingly, Jesus said that only those who could become "as a little child" could enter the kingdom of heaven. And development beyond "the new birth" is seen as "growing up into Christ."

Loneliness—Chained Curiosity

It occurs to me that man's *loneliness* is also tied into his curiosity. Those empty spots in his life are the results of unfulfilled wishes, unsatisfied needs, unaffirmed instincts, unrealized potentials, and uncertain directions in his person. This concept will be developed later, in the chapter on man's spirituality.

There is a need to "ask" in every man. He asks for information, for response, and for wish fulfillment.

Most of all, he asks for affirmation of who he is. When he hobbles the pony of curiosity, the pasture is too limited to raise a thoroughbred, the mature and fully developed animal. The man who no longer allows his queries to be expressed begins to accept the limits that ultimately result in death—the final break in his physical relationships.

Curiosity—Bondage or Freedom?

Let me tell you about Bob, a young man with much potential and a great curiosity about how he relates to his world. Bob sees himself as being aggressive and industrious in his working style, but he actually relates to people in a very passive and placating manner. He needs external assurance that he has the approval and affirmation of another person before he is able to move through a project successfully or before he is willing to make a decision. This puts a great deal of pressure on his wife. She is called upon to make most of the affirmations and reassurances that are necessary in his experience with the world.

But her support isn't always enough. In his immaturity and need for reassurance Bob allows his natural curiosity to develop into an insatiable desire for affirmation from new relationships. Because of this need he not only has an unsatisfactory vocational record, with numerous job changes, but he also allows this curiosity to feed his quest for female affirmation and to spur him into an affair with another woman. When I first saw Bob in counseling, he was unwilling to accept the child within him and was therefore prisoner to that child. Once he began to realize that it was acceptable for him to have feelings that he considered to be "childish" or immature, he began to grapple with that part of himself and to make progress in his life-style.

So many of us are afraid to accept any part of ourselves that we feel we cannot control, and in that lack of acceptance lies the loss of our freedom. For me, *freedom is the willingness to live even when I am not in control of the circumstances or situations of my life.* Freedom is also the possibility of facing things within myself that I may not like. It involves the willingness to engage in the struggle toward adjustment to tolerance of that attitude or behavior, through discipline or by a process of mental reconditioning.

When I'm unwilling to acknowledge to myself those things about which I am uncertain or insecure, then I am more likely to avoid those feelings or situations where I'm not in control. Acknowledging the inner child, therefore, sustains my possibilities for growth by giving me the freedom to enter new or difficult situations.

Duets of Discovery

People rarely discover anything while backing up. The freedom to risk forging ahead brings a special reward. It works in relationships too.

When we fear others, we "wall them out." When we reach for others, we "bridge" to them. Men and women make those choices toward each other. Introversion is an escape from others. In relationships, however, to escape within is to insulate our loneliness and increase our depression.

In college I had a roommate who was a loner. He was a brilliant student and rarely difficult as a living partner. He was afraid of people, especially females, until he met the girl who became his wife. Their romance, unseen by many because of their subtle exchanges, was like the blooming of a flower in the desert. Two quiet people, each secretly curious about the other, began to open themselves. They spanned a human chasm by their discovery of each other. A more demanding girl would have turned him further inward; a suave and sophisticated boy would have made her feel more inadequate. He found balance in her, and his life was never the same.

They explored together. He learned about a woman as she opened herself to him. My roommate needed time to become a man; he fortunately found a patient partner. Some men are not so fortunate!

4

ARE MEN
ALWAYS RIGHT?

*All rising to a great place
is by a winding stair.*

—Francis Bacon

In the early days of television there was an award-winning series called "Father Knows Best." It is still seen around the country in rerun versions on independent stations, even though the clothing and characters (like Robert Young) have changed a good deal. In looking at the character and development of men in our world, one continuing trouble is the "father knows best" syndrome. The patriarchal systems of family life have contributed an expectation that male responsibility is almost infallible.

Behind the Myth

I recently counseled a young couple struggling with the "men are always right" myth. In this family the wife appeared to be a very supportive, caring person. She told her children about her husband's prowess and apparently reinforced their level of appreciation for him. But as I worked with them it became apparent that this was her subtle way of avoiding responsibility in the family. By manipulating him into making most decisions, she was able to disavow any basic responsibility for the success or failure of the family system. Underneath the "father knows best" ideal was a working style that really meant "mother hides best."

As this couple began to examine their system, this attitude became quite apparent to them. They began to develop a new understanding of their roles. They progressed in their relationship by using various psychological inventories, particularly the one called

"Personality Characteristic Scale," a simple counseling tool I developed to help couples get in touch with their expectations of each other. Together we began to work systematically on changing the behavior that supports those expectations. They became eager learners as this basic and simple approach to system change in their relationship allowed for more responsibility for her and less "infallibility" for him.

I suggest that most marital systems change for only two reasons. One reason is that the pain of continuing in the kind of relationship the couple now has is so great that they are willing to do anything to bring about relief. The other is that the apparent rewards of a new way of relating look so inviting that one or both of them are willing to risk moving to the new kind of relationship. Those same reasons work for change in any individual's life.

Look at yourself. Are you supporting the "father knows best" system in your relationship with your wife and/or children? If so, the first step to begin to change that system, if you wish to, is to look at what you're getting out of the system. What reinforcement, what significant support is your internal man getting from your external behavior?

An Alternative Way

Tom's agenda was to build his own ego. He was willing to run the risk of the responsibilities of "always being right" in order to build himself up in the eyes of his associates, his family, and his friends. But he began to notice that he was getting into arguments and losing his temper, and, finally, failing to function sexually, which he blamed on his wife's inability to excite him. When he finally arrived in my office, pretty much unwillingly, he was close to desperation. His wife was ready to sue him for a divorce, and many of his business associates and social friends were supporting her in the action. His children were giving him signals that they were uncomfortable with his behavior and putting more distance between themselves and him in their day-to-day relationships.

He acted almost paranoid about his world in the early sessions. Soon he began to see that *his own defensive behavior* had contributed to his failing relationships. As he was gently reassured that there were other ways of relating that would work with people, he began to risk the possibility of "failure" in order to have a closeness in his relationships. Soon he and his wife started to listen to each other, and he began to develop a relationship with other people that was different. He began to risk being "wrong" in some of his judgments and allowing people to share with him in decisions that he made, rather than making a constant attempt to have an authoritative answer in every circumstance. He felt his life radically changing. I saw him giving up a phony idea of manhood and accepting a more realistic view of himself.

Being a man is not always being right! *Sometimes being a man is the ability to acknowledge that one has failed or is wrong about something.* That's a hard lesson for most of us to learn. But acknowledging failure is not a debit on the masculinity scale; it's a credit!

Self-protecting defenses—those methods of hiding from people—are the mechanisms that divert our attention from our fears. After awareness of what's happening to us, the second step in the process of growth is acknowledging to someone else what we know about ourselves.

I am more a man when I can face my inadequacies than when I must run from them. I think that's an important key to relating to women confidently. There's more to come on that subject.

5

WHO'S THE LUCKY GIRL?

At the heart of love there is a simple secret:
the lover lets the beloved be free.

—Kennedy

She complained that he should be ready by now. Her problem was a marriage—more specifically, marriage to a certain man. When I met her man, I understood more of her problem.

"How do I know she's the one I should marry?" he asked. "Bachelorhood has been awfully good to me." His question deserved careful thought from me and deliberation for himself. At thirty, he had been quite independent of women. "I know how to date a girl," and he described the intricate details of an evening he was planning. "Women are a fantastic challenge—until you get them—then they are a burden!"

Bob made me think a lot about why men and women marry. He knew the traditional answers as well as I did. It would please his parents and hers! The church would bless his union. He could settle down and spend less energy looking for dates.

He had gotten engaged the way many young people do—without *serious* thought. But as the wedding date drew nearer, panic set in! And weddings are enough to frighten most men.

If you don't believe this is a woman's world, look closely at our marriage rituals. There she is in all her glory, and there he is—nervous! Her "catch" is on display for all the world (gathered in that church) to see. Probably nobody feels more like an extra thumb than the groom at a wedding rehearsal or ritual.

In a more serious vein, the divorce rate reflects the invalidity of many of the serious "vows" we take. Almost half our marriages in the United States end in divorce. Many of those statistics are young people who marry much too soon—at least before they are ready to make that decision.

Men and women should have "butterflies" on their wedding days. They are making major decisions, many of them at a time when they know so little about themselves. Can we wonder that many marriages fail when couples decide between the ages of 17 and 24 with whom they may share a lifelong adventure? Is a man prepared to make that decision at that age? The answer is usually no. How can he cope with the question of marriage ability?

Marriage Ability

When is a man ready for marriage? I dare not suggest an all inclusive answer to the question. However, some "points to ponder" before that decision may be in order.

Using the biblical story of creation, there are insights about when a man is ready for marriage. Adam needed time to know himself, then time to know his needs, and time to accept Eve. To apply these to modern men requires some imagination but can be done. Let's try.

You are only ready to marry when you know who you are. That's a major requirement, but I want to soften it in two ways. No man ever fully knows *all* about himself if he is growing; obviously there is going to be more that he will know as he grows into that self knowledge. The basic self knowledge that prepares us for marriage is the elemental personal awareness. It begins with setting aside the fear of self-discovery and realistically beginning to assess my own strength and weaknesses.

The men I see who have decided to divorce their wives are often those who do not yet know themselves. Sometimes they believe a divorce is necessary because of what they have come to know about themselves. They now see themselves as incompatible with the expectations that they brought into the relationship with their present marital partner. Marriage involves basic adjustments and much compromise. The clearer your picture of yourself, the better your opportunity to adjust to marriage. To know yourself is a complex process, but there are some historical guidelines in the language of philosophy, psychology, and sociology. You can begin to know yourself by examining your thoughts, feelings, actions, and interactions with others.

Basic Elements

Intellect, emotion, and will interplay in our behavior and effect our responses from others. To limit the scope to marriage, ask yourself what you know, how you feel, and how you can decide on it. Discuss with some happily married people as well as some who are divorced what they see as being keys to the successes and failures of their relationships. Listen to their ideas and share your views. Read several books —some by male and some by female authors. As you express your ideas and raise questions, you will come to know yourself. Break down the things that you learn about yourself into the categories of intellectual ideas, emotional feelings, and discipline-making or decision-making processes. The intellectual aspects of you take on conceptual or theoretical form. They will usually follow most easily the phrase "I think. . . ." I *think* in facts, ideas, opinions, and data. I *feel* in emotional terms which have validity but which often defy factual, data, or conceptual containment. I *behave* through a combination of my thoughts and feelings in which I choose to act or react in certain ways. To some degree, all behavior is selected, established, and maintained by my will. In choosing a marriage partner, therefore, I need to examine carefully the data that I am feeding to my will about that decision.

Take Time to See

Particularly note your strengths and weaknesses as you consider a specific woman for your life. Do the two of you complement each other, or are you both similar in temperament? Quite often in premarital counseling I use a testing instrument called the Taylor-Johnson Temperament Analysis as a way of helping prospective marriage partners see how they view each other. Many counselors and ministers are prepared to help a couple prior to engagement to consider these questions. Premarital counseling with your intended is a tremendous investment in the potential future marriage. Time is on your side—use it well! Utilize all the resources available to you as an individual and as a couple.

Made in Heaven?

Probably every bride and bridegroom have some doubts on their wedding day and afterwards. Time is the only healer of these doubts. As you share a loving relationship, assurance grows and marital love deepens. For me, there was a sense of divine guidance in choosing a marriage partner. As surely as Eve came from the hand of God to Adam, a man may ask God for help in his search for a wife. The other day I ran across a poem given me by a high school girlfriend that applies here:

Dear wise and loving God above,
Show me the girl that I should love.
May she be good and kind and true;
May she have faith and believe in You.

Grant her a smile for each tomorrow;
May she have wisdom and joy and sorrow.
Let her have faults, dear Lord; you see,
I don't want her too much better than me!

May she be steady, firm, and sure,
That the hardships of life she may endure.
But this above all, Dear God, I ask,
As I give you this task—

First, Dear Lord, she must love you,
And then may she find she loves me too.

When a man discovers the love of a woman who will share his life, there is no surpassing joy for him. He is no longer alone to face life. His rewards, shared with her, multiply, and his sorrows, lightened by her concern, divine. Depending upon the level of your spiritual development, you may sense an awareness of God's leading you to a special girl for your life. If you don't feel particularly spiritually attuned, it may be a good time to begin. Marriage is so important; you can use all the help you can get!

But don't forget my friend Bob; he wanted to know if *this* girl was the one who would share his life, double his happiness, and divide his sorrows. I didn't know. How could he decide?

Stop, Look, and Listen

The old adage is "Look at her mother!" That's not bad advice. But as you may not be limited to the input from your parents, she may have other people who have helpfully or destructively influenced her. Looking at your potential mother-in-law will give you a pretty good idea about the strong influences in your chosen one's life. She is more likely to either model the behavior of her mother or to rebel against the model her mother has provided.

I asked Bob four questions: Who have you known before like her? What are her basic personality characteristics? How does she handle stress situations? What are her goals for the future? Try them on for size in your life.

The first question is directed at your understanding of the relationship to your own mother. The more the woman you choose is like your mother, beware! Unresolved dependency may be hidden like a landmine in your marital path. There may also loom a power struggle where your maternal rebellions can be extended. Without overanalyzing, the biggest problem in choosing a woman like your mother may be your relationship to your father. You may really be living out what you need to tell him about your observations of his way of relating to your own mother. He's already had a chance to live his life; don't try to correct his mistakes in your life. Be thorough in exploring this question—you may avoid much future grief.

The question about her basic personality characteristics is vital. Is she an "open" person? Do you feel relaxed around her? Is she easy to be with over an extended period of time? Does she "wear well" in a relationship; that is, do you like her more as you know more about her? If she is "closed" and responds only to your direct questions, there will probably come a time when you will feel very isolated from her in marriage. If you see her as being "handled with kid gloves," better try on those gloves for size. If you don't like the fit, get out of the store! A good rule is that you won't change her after you are married. So don't overlook what could be a source of infection to the relationship. Surgery is always possible to relieve the pressure of that infection, but it brings its own pain. Preventive action is preferable to repair work in all health fields, including marital health!

How does she handle stress? She may handle it (such as the excessive use of alcohol, cigarettes, pills) well and that can threaten your "male ego." She may "fall apart" when she doesn't get her way. She may be an "escape artist"—avoiding any unpleasant reality by running away. This failure to face up to situations can be seen in stoic denial, habitual reflexes etc., or in literal physical movements away from sources of stress. Running from her family to you is probably an avoidance pattern, so stop, look, and listen! If she is extremely critical of her parents and acquaintances, how long do you think it will be until you join her disapproval list?

Finally, compare your life goals. If you like to roam, does she? Wanderlust turns to resentment when you feel she is "holding you back," particularly if your career is involved. Has she planned for several children while you don't really want them? Is the style of life you plan to offer one she can find acceptable for the future? Look into the mirror of the future and imagine what life with her would be like five years or ten years from now. If you are not satisfied with what you see, apply the brakes now.

Love alone won't conquer *all* things. Marriage is a cooperative effort. It is not two looking into each other's eyes—though romance continues—it is two standing shoulder to shoulder looking ahead toward the same goals. You can only work together to attain those goals that you can both see. If this chapter troubles you, go slowly in your commitments to marriage.

For more on your journey, let's look at the keys to her kingdom.

PART 2

DISCOVERING THE WORLD OF WOMEN

*It is possible
to give away and become richer!
It is also possible
to hold on too tightly
and lose everything.*

—Proverbs 11:24, *The Living Bible*

6

WELCOME TO MY WORLD!

*I love you, not only for what you have
made of yourself,*
But for what you are making of me.

*I love you because you have done more
than any creed to make me happy.*

You have done it without a word, without a touch, without a sign,
Just by being yourself.

After all, perhaps that is what love is.

Once you were expelled from the inner recesses of a woman; for many men life's mission seems to be to regain entry to her magic kingdom. For others the world of women is as threatening and mysterious as the birth process itself.

Women are becoming more aggressive about their sexual needs.

In the last four or five years I have been seeing more husbands whose wives have either manipulated or dragged them into my office. For many years I think it could be safely said that sex was considered to be a male domain. The stereotyped "nice" woman was not interested in sex. With the arrival of more openness about sexuality, and with the advent of the liberation movement specifically, women have been demanding more fulfillment of the sexual needs in their lives. Since the sexual revolution began and the Masters and Johnson studies hit the public, men have found out that women could express themselves sexually more than we knew. Some men are intimidated by this knowledge. Often a man temporarily or occasionally becomes impotent as a result of greater sexual demands by his female partner. The resultant problem is an increase in the number of cases of primary and secondary impotence.

Let me define my terms for a moment. Primary impotence is the inability of the male partner to achieve erection; secondary impotence is the inability to achieve or maintain erection to a point where he or his female partner is able to gain satisfaction from the sexual experience they share. With this definition, of course, I include premature ejaculation as a part of secondary impotence. The premature ejaculation of the semen and sperm into the vagina of the female, leaving her unsatisfied, is a failure or an inadequacy on the part of the male to bring sexual satisfaction to his female partner.

Minds Motivate Matter

It would be easy with this definition to launch into the physical aspect of the relationship. However, in terms of importance, the most important gift that a man has to offer a woman sexually is not his penis. It is not his knowledge of her anatomy. It is something else. The most important part of himself that a man can give a woman is his *mind*. The sexually adequate man is first of all stimulating in what he thinks about a woman. The "Don Juan" or "Casanova" of the world has been that man who has been able to make a woman feel that, while with her, she was the only woman in the world.

To make a woman feel special begins with how you think about her, what you expect of her, what you sense about her, how you hear her—actually, how you project your thoughts about her. All of that is "mind" sexuality! If you stop for a moment to think how it is with the woman in your life, you may find yourself coming up short! If you are critical of her, if you have been expressing your disappointment with her, if you have described her body as being somewhat less than attractive to you—if these are the

61

kinds of thoughts that have been filling your mind, then it is going to be very difficult for you to be a sexually stimulating, adequate male. The beginning point of the "turn on" in the woman in your life is between your ears, not between your legs. What you think about her, how you feel about her, and the way you communicate that to her is most important.

A few years ago I counseled a man involved in an affair. Affairs are not unusual, but this particular man said to me, "*She* is so different from my wife. My wife is inhibited; this woman is sexually liberated. My wife has an average body; the woman I'm having an affair with has an exquisite body. My wife is a good mother, but the woman that I'm having the affair with is an excellent mother: she takes care of her children, etc., etc." He described the way this woman responded to him sexually, and as he talked he told me about the difference in his life since he had met her. I pointed out to him that he *expected* her to be this excellent person. He *expected* her to be exquisite and he *expected* her to be an amorous partner in bed. In many ways she was simply living up to his expectations. I suggested that before he decided there was no hope for continuing the relationship he had with his wife, he might first examine his expectations of his wife.

An interesting thing happened. As this man began to see the reasoning I was suggesting, he made a temporary commitment to his wife that he would do the best he could to expect from her the kinds of things that he had been expecting from the woman with whom he had had the affair. It was almost like a miracle! The next time he came into my office, he said things were changing in their relationship; his wife, who had been described as sexually inhibited, was becoming a sexual tiger in bed! Something was happening to her. But it was in *his* mind! He was expecting her to be more adequate, more sexual during this time of new commitment in his life, and she was living up to his expectations!

I don't want to say that every time a husband or a wife is having an affair, all it takes is for one of them to simply begin to think differently about their relationship and it will change. There is, however, truth in the statement that if people will begin to *think* differently about each other, the *behavior* that they share with each other will also change greatly.

Open Your Mind to Her

It is not enough just to think expectantly about the woman in your life. The world is full of great poets who never got the words out of their minds, so we don't know who they are. The world has many unpublished "great" novels which were never put on paper. It is important that a man recognize that the next most significant thing he has to offer a woman, if he is to be a sexually adequate male, in his *mouth*!

First, his mouth is an instrument of verbal communication. It *tells* her how he is feeling, what's happening in his head, what he is expecting from her, what he is sensing, what he is admiring, and what he is experiencing in the relationship with her. Words are awfully important. One of the big complaints I hear from women is that men rarely say "I love you" unless they are in the middle of intercourse. "He never tells me I'm pretty unless he is ready for us to go to bed." "He never says I'm attractive unless he's got that gleam in his eye, and I know what that means." Sound familiar?

It is important for you to share with your woman what you are thinking about her and what you are thinking about life. A part of being a sexually adequate male is being able to *share intimacy* with the woman in your life. Open up your inner world to her and let her know what you are thinking and feeling. Being able to share with her your "heart" is letting her in on the "inner space" of your life. She becomes a mental astronaut and orbits your world, breaking through into the spacious areas where you have not allowed anyone to go, that you have guarded with the force of your defenses and protectiveness. Invite her in, share with her who you really are, and you will be surprised at the kind of closeness that will result between you. Your mouth is important because you can choose words that tell her how you feel—and speak them with feeling, with depth, with dignity. Sometimes we say the right words but our tone belies us or our facial expressions say something else. I first get in touch with my own feelings, then I am able to speak them clearly to the woman in my life. Don't expect her to be a mind reader; tell her how you feel about her!

The Mouth Makes Music

Second, the mouth is important because it is a very special instrument of lovemaking. Kissing, tonguing, caressing her body with your mouth is a tender and gentle way of expressing your feelings about your wife. I hear often from women who are sexually dissatisfied, "He doesn't appear to like to kiss me. It is just a peck on the cheek. There are no passionate embraces and lingering kisses; no more of the deep, probing kinds of kisses that used to mark our courtship." The kiss is a symbol of a special kind of intimacy, particularly the deep and intimate passionate kiss. It is important for us to be sensitive to the needs of the female in our lives as well as our own needs. Learn to express your feelings gently and tenderly through the lips. Experiment with your lips as an erotic sensitizer of other parts of her body. One of the discoveries that many nonorgasmic women are making is that their first sexual climax occurs through oral stimulation. It is essential then for a man to be willing to stimulate his wife's body with his mouth in order for her to gain total sexual pleasure and for him to be an adequate sexual partner.

Before you decide that mouth stimulation is not for you, remember that your earliest contacts with a woman's body were oral. There is a special sense of well-being for many women in having their breasts kissed and sucked. It is not true for all women. Nor will all appreciate other oral contacts. Offer her your mouth for her pleasure—she will let you know her limits. And her pleasure is your goal; the greatest lover never loses sight of his beloved's needs.

The Gift of Your Hands

The third major piece of equipment for the sexually adequate male is his *hands*. The beginning place for many sexual therapy programs is the use of massage. Sensory-awareness experiences, in which couples are asked to touch each other, are ways of encouraging them to talk about their feelings about touch. We have too often eliminated the gentle, tender, and strong touches from our relationships. How long has it been since you gave your wife a massage, starting with her head and massaging her body all the way down to her toes—front and back? You may communicate more intimacy, more appreciation, and more sensitivity through your hands than you realize. I ask husbands and wives to use their hands when they are becoming sensitized to feelings and needs for each other—gentle finger-tapping and gentle touching of the fingertips on the face and on the rest of the body in sensual exercise. I describe this exercise and ask the husband and wife to use it at home for more erotic pleasure and more sexual fulfillment in their relationship. To be a more sexually adequate man, use your mind, your mouth, and your hands! Be creative—the rewards are mind-boggling!

Your Instrument of Love

Finally, the part of himself that a man can give a woman is the special instrument that God has created for the male—his *penis*. Remember that this is the fourth instrument the sexually adequate male has to offer! And the most important thing to the woman in your life is not how large your penis is, how big it gets, or how long you can keep it erect! The most important thing to her is that your penis is an instrument of loving.

The sexually adequate man, in my judgment, is not penis-centered. Many men in our society are self-centered and, to put it in the vernacular, "hung up" about the size of their penises or how they can function sexually. As I see it, the sexually adequate male could function even if he were missing his penis because of the importance of the other three gifts he has to give a woman—his mind, his mouth, and his hands. Loving expressions, loving feelings, and sharing with each other as you grow older in your marital life need not be curtailed because of the decreasing ability to function, which occurs in some, not all, men.

Intimacy Grows

The sexual experience between a man and a woman is the highest form of intimacy that the human being can know. A whole man is able to use the totality of what he knows about himself to seek more adequate and rewarding experiences in sex, just as he does about other aspects of his life. I'd like to make some suggestions for you to build a more sexually adequate relationship with your partner.

First, a more adequate sexual relationship must be based on *empathy*—being sensitive to her needs, her feelings, and her desires. A TV commercial says something like this: "Want him to be more of a man? Try being more of a woman!" The opposite also holds true. Remember, the more you are aware of the needs of your sexual partner, the more you empathize with her feelings, the more you remind her and help her to feel that she is a special woman, the more you are going to feel like a man. You will experience more of the satisfaction you want in your relationship. You will strengthen that relationship by communicating that empathy, by sharing your feelings with her. A growing sexual relationship is built on a "relationship-centered motivation" as compared to a self-centered one. A growing relationship is one where both partners are able to give and to receive.

An adequate, growing sexual relationship is also based upon what we might call *self-governorship*—the capacity of each person in the relationship to govern his or her own actions in the interest of their relationship. To please your sexual partner is not to placate her. Significant is the ability to feel a sense of *identification* and *love* for your partner in the relationship.

Also important for a growing sexual relationship is

a *freedom of expression.* There are never times when you and your partner must compromise with honest expression of feelings, or else genuine communication will be removed from your sexual relationship. All possible taboos that you can list need to be dealt with and handled in an open way. Loving honesty is always the best procedure!

Making Changes

If you are not satisfied with where you are in the relationship that you share with the woman in your life, first of all begin by *taking stock of yourself.* List on a piece of paper (1) what parts of our relationship am I happy with and (2) what parts do I want to change. (It is important for you to write down the things that you are thinking so that you can look at them and, in a healthy way, "talk back" to yourself.) Then sit down with that woman in your life and *tell her* about your feelings, frustrations, fears, and anxieties. Express appreciation to her for the ways that she has been patient with you, if that is applicable. Begin to communicate with her what your hopes are for the relationship. If this attempt toward a better sexual relationship fails and if the two of you want to communicate more effectively, don't be afraid to seek professional help. Today people are trained to work in the area of sexual therapy.*

* You can get a referral for this kind of therapist from the national office of the American Association of Marriage and Family Counselors, 225 Yale Avenue, Claremont, California 91711. The phone number is (714) 624-4749. Beware of dealing with a person who is not well-trained and certified by an appropriate professional organization.

7

BE SELFISH!
KEEP GROWING!

*Discovery consists in
seeing what everybody else has seen
and thinking what nobody else thought.*

Think of the growing male as a man who is first concerned with knowing himself. As I read accounts of therapy experiences in my supervision program, I'm impressed with the ability of marital pairs to blame each other for what happens in their relationship. A woman will say, "My husband is not satisfying me sexually" or "My husband is not paying enough attention to me; he doesn't care!"

Sometimes the accusations are true. This book is not written to exonerate husbands. It is an attempt to focus attention in the direction of the possible progress in the face of the problems. If a man is going to be a growing person, moving toward more adequacy in the total fulfillment of his humanity, he must first begin with *himself*. He cannot be preoccupied with his wife and her problems or with his children and their problems; he must first learn who *he* is. In my experience with troubled marriages, one of the most helpful kind of things that happens is when both partners are able to move away from their problems for a moment and begin to get a chance to see *who they are*, without condemnation! This very often happens in a process that I call a Personal Growth Group.

Share and Grow

In the Personal Growth Group one of the first things we do is to begin to teach a person how to share himself with others. He learns to disclose himself. He reveals, by choice, some of his inner being to new friends. So if a man is to know himself and be a growing male the first step is to disclose himself to others. The late Sidney Jourard has rightfully pointed out that until a person shares himself with others he cannot really know himself fully. In Everett Shostrom, Virginia Satir, Abraham Maslow, Carl Rogers, and others, the concept is reiterated that the actualizing person—the person who is becoming whole, fully developing his unique talents and abilities—is the one who is able to share himself and his insights with others.

This contradicts our common assumptions about men. Men are cool; they keep their thoughts to themselves; they don't go to others for opinions or advice, unless, of course, it is about buying stock! They don't share their emotions with other people. Men isolate themselves to avoid sharing feelings! Of course, these descriptions are stereotyped, and these unrealistic stereotypes conflict with what a man may really want.

To be adequate a man must be able to acknowledge, to articulate, and to accept who he *is*. His first step is to become more honest with *himself*. Then he begins to share his openness with *other people*. This is difficult to do with his family and others who are very close to him. It may be helpful for him to find, under professional guidance, a group of strangers in which to begin this process.

Characteristics of Growth

Let's assume for a moment that you are beginning the process of self-disclosing. What are some of the characteristics of the "total man"? One is *assertiveness*! A whole man is willing to give leadership. Notice that I did not say dominance! Assertiveness and dominance are two different things. One can be assertive, offer leadership, and be aggressive without necessarily dominating. He can be assertive and negotiate. He does not have to be totally in control when he is assertive.

How does a man assert his leadership? The New Testament calls this the "headship" of the husband. How can you offer this to the female in your life without being overly dominant? You can easily pass from the leadership to the dictatorial side! But if you are going to be an adequate male, you do what Charlie Shedd suggests to his son in his *Letters to Phillip*. You take charge! That does not mean that you make decisions without consideration for the feelings of the woman in your life, but it does mean that you are willing to accept the responsibility and to exercise the authority that is yours as part of the relationship.

Let me balance this by saying that a growing male is *aware*. He is aware of himself through the process of self-disclosure but he is also aware of others. He is sensitive and responds to the needs of others—particularly to the needs of the woman in his life. He shows his awareness by his willingness to listen as much as he talks. This sensitivity will often preclude verbal explanations by communicating understanding non-verbally.

Leadership in a relationship is not giving orders, answers, or explanations. Leadership may often be providing the kind of quiet stability that another person needs to feel trusted. It says, "I have confidence in your ability to make decisions." This leadership encourages others to act because you have given them the courage, the opportunity, and the strength to do so through your awareness of their needs and potential. A wife can be less dependent and less troubled by her dependence if the man in her life is able to express confidence in her abilities. He is sensitive to her need for that confidence to be expressed.

Another characteristic of the full man is *courage*—to stand alone, to call himself a man. I am reminded of Rudyard Kipling's famous poem, "If":

If you can keep your head when all about you
    Are losing theirs and blaming it on you;
If you can trust yourself when all men doubt you,
    But make allowance for their doubting too;
If you can wait and not be tired by waiting,
    Or, being lied about, don't deal in lies,
Or, being hated, don't give way to hating,
    And yet don't look too good, not talk too wise;

If you can dream—and not make dreams your master;
If you can think—and not make thoughts your aim;
If you can meet with triumph and disaster

And treat those two impostors just the same;
If you can bear to hear the truth you've spoken
    Twisted by knaves to make a trap for fools,
Or watch the things you gave your life to broken,
    And stoop and build 'em up with wornout tools;

If you can make one heap of all your winnings
    And risk it on one turn of pitch-and-toss,
And lose, and start again at your beginnings
    And never breathe a word about your loss;
If you can force your heart and nerve and sinew
    To serve your turn long after they are gone,
And so hold on when there is nothing in you
    Except the will which says to them, "Hold on";

If you can talk with crowds and keep your virtue,
    Or walk with kings—nor lose the common touch;
If neither foes nor loving friends can hurt you;
    If all men count with you, but none too much;
If you can fill the unforgiving minute
    With sixty seconds' worth of distance run—
Yours is the earth and everything that's in it,
    And—which is more—you'll be a man, my son!
                                    —Rudyard Kipling

Sometimes we cannot fully respect ourselves until we say, as Martin Luther did in one of the great challenges of his life, "Here I stand; I can do no other; God help me!" A man decides what his convictions are and has the courage to stand by them!

Closely aligned to his convictions, however, is the

characteristic of *positiveness*. A growing man, in my judgment, is a man who is able to accept things about himself and about others with hope. He is genuinely happy because he has a direction for his life. He is positive in expressing this growth.

The growing man is *enthusiastic*. There is a great power in enthusiasm. When you look positively and enthusiastically at any situation, you can give leadership to your family. As an example, you leave work bone weary, tired from problems you've been facing all day, looking forward to peace and quiet. But you step into the house and suddenly it seems that nothing is going right. Before long you and your wife are into an argument and the children are in an uproar with each other. You wish you hadn't even come home. It's just more pressure! Then, as the facts begin to unfold, you are surprised and chagrined.

Your wife had fixed your favorite meal. Your children were ready and anxious to share their day with you when you came home from the office. But, because you were tired and down in the dumps, when you stepped into the house you set a tone that infected all of them. They had looked forward expectantly for your arrival but soon everyone was hurt and disappointed. Your enthusiasm would have taken a bad situation at home and changed it.

It happens in your office or other situations in your world. If you have the responsibility of motivating people, you know that you often have to enthuse them if they are going to do the special job that you want. It is also true with your wife or your family.

Give the kind of enthusiastic and appreciative leadership that they need in the family. It will flow back in your direction!

I see the growing man as being *warm* and *tender*. All genuine strength has within it tenderness, and all true tenderness has within it genuine strength. A man need not be afraid of his emotions. He need not hesitate to express his feelings to the woman in his life. He needs to begin to share himself for her to believe that she is really important to him and that he needs her. She is affirmed by his openness. His willingness to risk with her assures her of his love and concern for their intimacy.

Weakness or Strength

One of the fascinating experiences I have in therapy is to take weaknesses that people express about themselves and help them to discover strengths in the midst of those weaknesses. I ask a husband and wife to list all of the negatives they know about each other and then attempt to express a positive aspect of each of the negatives. For example, a wife may say, "You are a stubborn man." After looking at that quality closely she may be able to say, "I'm thankful for your determination and ability to stick to something once you have made up your mind."

Or a man may describe himself as indecisive. "I find it difficult to make choices when opinions are differing around me." As he examines that statement he may discover a positive attribute in that he is able to listen to all the facts and perhaps be a conciliator, a person who is able to work out compromise when persons around him are holding decisively to their opinions.

Try this with yourself as you begin to learn who you are. Make a list of all the things that you consider to be weaknesses about yourself. See if you can find a way to describe some positive strengths within what you list as weaknesses. Emphasize the positive within your own life. You are a whole person when you will allow yourself to live out the wholeness within you. If you allow yourself to live only within certain limitations, then you will be living out only part of what you are. But if you are unafraid to face *all* of yourself, you will discover that you are engaging in the process of wholeness, of self-actualization.

Being an adequate man does not mean that you always have the answers! We focus too much on Dad's being "the man who knows everything." Being a loving and adequate man means that you can accept your failures. It means that, at times, you acknowledge being wrong. You don't *always* have to be right: I think the growing man is open to this kind of change; he is not so fixated on one position that he cannot accept other people's views and ideas. You are not locked into a form of manipulative behavior. You can therefore free yourself from the position of being the judge or the bully. You can become free from the calculating and dictating positions in which you must connive, trying always to find a way to keep yourself from being blamed and to do "the right thing" in a set of circumstances or a context. It means that you can be free of placating—you don't always have to be the "nice guy" or the "protector" who keeps other people from knowing how you feel and concentrates solely on them, never really allowing your own feelings to emerge.

Being an adequate man means that you can be freed from *avoidance behavior*. You need not be the clinging vine who is indecisive and who needs someone to tell him what he ought to do. You can escape the position of the weakling who is a "yes" man to the decisions of others. You need not avoid making quips or comments, but never being serious about what is happening in your own life reflects a distracting life-style.

The adequate man need not manipulate because he is able to begin to face himself as he really is. He will discover that as he gives respect to others, a growing respect for himself from others will result! He will find that as he loves others, love will truly be returned, with satisfaction for himself.

Don't Cheat Yourself

I'm impressed with how many men fail themselves in the process of discovering and exercising their total manhood. It reminds me of one of Edward Markham's stories which he calls "The Parable of the Builder." As I recall, the story is about a king who had a carpenter over whom he ruled. Before the king set out on a journey, he said to his carpenter, "I want you to build a fine house." He indicated the location on a sunny slope across from the palace. The king gave him the contract to build the house and left on his journey.

While the king was gone, the carpenter decided that this was an opportunity to do something deceitful. He would build shabbily. The house would have an excellent appearance but he could make a lot of money by using shoddy materials. Before the king discovered the trick the carpenter could move and successfully deceive the king. Soon the house was finished, and the carpenter heard that the king was returning. He took the keys to the king's palace, ready to show the king through the new house. They stood on the palace veranda and looked at the house gleaming in the sunlight. And the carpenter thought how shrewd he had been.

Then the king said to him, "You have been a faithful carpenter in my kingdom all these years, and I want to reward you in some way. I asked you to build this house so that I could give it to you. It is a fine house built with your own hands in which you can live out your days in my kingdom. It is my gift to you!" You can imagine how crestfallen the man was! He had industriously cheated himself out of a beautiful home that could have been his own absolutely free.

Many men these days cheat themselves out of being a total man because of their own fears, the expectations of others, the demands of their parents, or other rationalizations. But they are cheating themselves! When life is over, there will be some sad men who are unable to experience all that was intended for their lives because they were unwilling to follow the basic steps for wholeness and satisfaction.

8

ROOKIE OF THE YEAR

If you give a man a fish,
you feed him for a day;
if you teach a man how to fish,
you feed him for life.

—Chinese Proverb

One of the places I lived in as a boy was in Florida. Near Clearwater the New York Yankees, the Philadelphia Phillies, and several other major league baseball teams had winter training camps. I remember as a youngster seeing Babe Ruth, after his playing days, sitting in the stands watching the younger players and commenting on their potential and their possibilities for the future. It was always a thrill for me to meet a new young ball player in the winter league training camp and then to discover during the season and perhaps at the conclusion of his first season of the year that he was being considered for the title "Rookie of the Year!"

As I thought about being a rookie, it occurred to me that almost every year of my life I have in some ways felt like a "rookie." When I was just a little man I was learning how to relate to my world. Next I learned how to relate to the educational system, then to the socialization and courtship systems. Then came the world of college and vocational choices. That step led to initial jobs, marriage, and fatherhood! One step barely gets comfortable when another step is required. And at almost every level there is really no adequate way of preparing for the *next* level at which we are asked to perform. In some ways we can never *stop* being rookies!

A rookie's major problem is the problem of survival. He doesn't have the settled place on the team, and he must constantly "hustle" if he is going to keep this position or earn a starting berth in the lineup. Much of the pressure that a man feels in his life is like that of being a rookie; he is constantly working to survive.

Survival and Meaning

Some years ago I read a study of churches in the San Francisco Bay area. I was impressed by the author's description of churches and institutions going through two stages—the *survival* stage and the *meaning* stage. When you're struggling for survival, it's very difficult to ask questions about meaning.

When a man marries, he may have his mind made up to be the "Rookie of the Year" as far as being a marriage partner is concerned. His attempt will probably last well through the honeymoon and into the first year of the marriage. However, he soon discovers, as does his wife, that there are certain demands which the two of them must meet if they are going to survive in the wonderful world of newlywed bliss! Too often the young husband becomes bogged down in making a living or, perhaps even worse, his career begins to skyrocket and he becomes absorbed in each new success. He may truly be a "sensational" young man on the scene as far as his company is concerned, but it may be that this success causes his greatest failure—the relationship with his wife.

He becomes preoccupied with his need to survive at the next level and he moves up quickly. The old adage "success breeds success" is probably true, but it often also breeds personal distancing in relationships. This growing distance between husband and wife is the result of his preoccupation with his career and his success. He finds it so easy to justify. After all, she will be proud of him! He wants to please her and to provide for her all the good things that they together dream about.

It all happens so innocently. Now they are able to afford to have the baby they had hoped for. She becomes pregnant, and soon she is staying at home while he is working long hours, and the loneliness in both of them grows. He begins to feel pressure, physical fatigue, and even a sense of her dependence on him for some contact with the outside world. She begins to feel more restricted and less satisfied, and she senses somehow that he is "slipping away" from her.

As her possessiveness increases, his defensiveness and elusiveness build. Then they begin to ask the fatal question. What does our relationship mean? By this time they have usually reached the sixth to ninth years of their marriage and the "rut" has gotten deep. Perhaps a second child is now in the picture. There is more and more necessity for "surviving" and less and less reason for asking "why." But underneath it all there are more demands to seek meaning and less motivation to continue to survive without knowing the answers. Frustration sets in, and the "perfect marriage" begins to become the impossible dream.

Self-Protective Systems

What's happened to our "Rookie of the Year"? Let me give you examples of ways in which men cope with this kind of crisis in their lives. First look at Joe. Joe is 28 years of age, a fairly successful young vice-president in his company. He has been married eight years and has two children, and the gloss of his relationship to his wife and to his job has really worn off.

I'll Follow You

As his mechanism of defense against this transition period in his life, Joe chooses what psychologists call *introjection*. He takes into himself the feelings and emotions of other people. The most important person whom he seeks to emulate is his boss. This means he is a great "company man." His boss wears gray suits to work; Joe wears gray suits to work. His boss joins the country club; Joe joins the country club. His boss drinks; Joe drinks. His boss acts nonchalant about his relationship to his wife, and Joe acts nonchalant in his relationship to his wife. Joe becomes almost a carbon copy of the person he is using as a pattern for his life. This is one example of introjection.

He may also emulate his wife! Some couples become so much alike that it's hard to tell them apart. My thesis on this kind of "similarity" marriage, however, is that when two people agree on everything one of them is unnecessary! A carbon copy really adds nothing to the original; it only reminds us of what the original was like. When another person patterns his life after his partner, his boss, or any other individual to the point that he has nothing left which is uniquely his own, then his life is really a waste—unnecessary.

Everything Is Beautiful

Let's look at Frank. Frank is what we would call a *denier*. Frank pretends that everything is great in his life, that there is no question of survival. There has been no survival period; there is no "meaning" period going on in his life. He and his wife have been married for twelve years. They have never had a fuss or a fight, and everything is wonderful, yet Frank is denying reality. Soon his denial will show up—perhaps in the form of ulcers, migraine headaches, or some other physical symptoms.

Frank's need to keep himself charged up under these circumstances will become even greater. As a defense he will find himself needing to invest in causes and circumstances which will prove that everything is not like his "gut" tells him it is. He gets busy; he works hard. He does all the things he is supposed to do and he becomes a tremendous achiever. But achieving doesn't answer his questions.

It's Later Than I Thought

Another kind of defense in which a man may engage at this point is what psychologists call *regression*. He may revert to a previous level of functioning which is less than his normal level of behavior. He has a new romance in his life, which *could* mean he falls in love again with his wife or it could mean he has an affair with his secretary!

It could mean that he starts to "play." Very often when a man goes through what Edmund Bergler called "the revolt of the middle-aged man," he is regressing to an earlier form of behavior. He is a teenager again! He buys a red convertible. He adds some flashy new clothes to his wardrobe. He changes his hairstyle. He loses weight and seeks to change his physical appearance. All of this, which sometimes appears to be a way of "regaining his youth," is a regression back to an earlier form of behavior which our man is using to defend himself against the crisis in his life.

I Need a New Challenge

Another form of defense is *escapism*. Jack, at 29, had succeeded at being "Rookie of the Year," but he could sense that his days of being the new boy on the block would soon be over. So he jumped to a new level and tried to become the "sophomore sensation" in his line of business. He could have attempted escape by changing vocations at this point, by alcoholism, or by drugs. Sometimes a man tries to escape through another relationship. Or he might try to escape by burying himself in his work. In any case he is trying to run away from his feelings by escaping from the consequences of what he is doing. At best he postpones those consequences, but he never avoids them.

Comfortable Digression

A final form of defense is *fixation*. This idea has been popularized by such books as *The Peter Principle*. One can defend oneself against any crisis by simply staying at the level at which one has become comfortable. A man becomes a robot! He may function well but there is no way to go up and very little way that he can go back in his life. This often leads to severe depression. Harold was like that. Harold worked for a company in which he had achieved a certain level of expertise. There was no way for him to go higher in the company, as he saw it, but he had excellent job security. Then an awful depression hit him! He soon began to see that it was a result of his being fixated or trapped. His depression grew. When he finally came to me for help, before he could make any progress he had to give up the security of the comfortable level of his life in order to advance to a new level.

Perfectionist

Before I leave this emphasis on defenses against the crises that occur in our lives, let me mention one more pressure that a man can be under. Take Paul as an example. Paul is afraid of appearing "burned out" at forty. He has experienced great success in his line of work, but he often feels there is no place to go. He works hard at appearing alive with new ideas and new opportunities, when underneath he is struggling to see if there is really any satisfaction in the job that he is doing now.

He is a determined man, a perfectionist. I listened to Paul use the word "must" nearly one hundred times in the first two hours I saw him. He used the word so often that I began to pencil out a message on my notebook paper. It became *M*an *U*nder *S*tress and *T*ension. Again I wrote, *M*an *U*nloading *S*train and *T*error. The more I listened to the drive and the ambition in Paul, the more I heard the stress, fear, and terror.

Failing to constantly be achieving something new is the mark of the perfectionist—the driven man. He whips himself onward to the next level of achievement, the next goal. He has within himself an "insistent" parent (to use a transactional analysis term). Only what he fails to do has significance—what he has already accomplished fades quickly. Compulsively, he drives even harder toward the next project or challenge. But, sadly, he has no time to enjoy what he has achieved.

Fear of the Unknown

The specific threat of being a man in a woman's world is the challenge of *old expectations*. The woman's liberation movement has caused us to ask, "What are the things that 'men should do' and 'women should do'?" Some men are terribly threatened by the fall of "protected sanctuaries" like bars, men's clubs, etc. Other men are troubled by vocational assertiveness on the part of women who are taking over the kinds of jobs that they feel "only a man can do." If a man is going to deal with this kind of fear in himself, then he is going to have to ask himself, "Where does real security lie? Is it in what I do or is it in who I am?"

My strong suggestion is that *who* a man is determines *what* he does. And *who* a woman is determines *what* she does. If either of them "need" to prove something about themselves, they will attempt to make those impressions, those approvals, those "brownie points" as long as they live. There will always be "male strongholds" for some women to try to overcome, and there will always be some "protected sanctuaries" for some men to protect.

In Sarah Connelly's *The Unquiet Grave* is a line that succinctly states the issue: "Two fears alternate, the one of loneliness and one other of bondage." Whenever a man protects something by a barrier against the outside world, he also limits himself to the safety of that barrier. What I am unwilling to share with another person must be "enjoyed" in isolation!

A man who defines his world by things specifically masculine in orientation will live with a consuming fear of the female world. The converse is true for a woman. What is *different* from me has the potential of *threatening* me. Too many of us choose only to defend ourselves against the threat. We too seldom recognize the pleasure of exploration which exists in the unknown or the different in life.

A poster in my group room says "People are lonely because they build walls instead of bridges." A man is afraid of a woman's true self-liberation only because that kind of freedom inherently demands too much responsibility from him.

Only the man who knows himself comfortably can ever fully know a woman. That which I fear in myself and will not accept I will project on to another and despise.

The "Rookie" maturational period is marked by a knowledge of my strengths and my attempts to "sell" them to the world around me. As I mature in life, I am willing to face my limitations and to learn to live fully in spite of them. I don't fear my weakness when I know it better than anyone else. Maturity lessens fears and multiplies freedoms. Being a man is becoming mature!

9

BRAVE NEW WORLD

To love someone is
to give him room enough to grow.

There was a time I can remember when the worlds of men and women were clearly delineated. Perhaps it was in that era described recently by a TV commentator as "the good old days—when sex was dirty and air was clean!"

A subtle trend in the garment industry in the late 1960's emphasized the "pants suit," which is and will perhaps continue to be a strong part of the market in women's wear. "Unisex" themes in the dress of men and women appeared more frequently. Homosexual fashions became more open. While black liberation gained or waned, women's liberation took center stage. "I Am Woman" was a musical smash hit and a New York congresswoman waged a serious though futile campaign for the presidency of the United States. A woman governor was elected. "Male chauvinist pig" became a rallying cry for women liberationists and an honored brand for challenged men.

If that was the "fall season" of the forest of maleness and femaleness, surely after winter has passed with its stark bleakness, a new and glorious spring will dawn. Its signs are present in the winter of our discontent like the tiny flowers that break through the late snows of April in Minnesota.

Women have asserted themselves and all the men of the world have not fled to the seas. But adjustment is painful for some.

The Boss Is a Woman!

"I'm going to quit my job," he grumbled. "Why?" I queried, watching his hostility make his nose quiver. "I cannot work for that woman," Matt responded. "She is out of her place in that job." It was not hard to figure out that Matt's problem was not his new female boss, though he thought she was. We explored his world of fear during the next few sessions. Matt's fear of his future with a woman boss had all the elements of paranoia. He projected his own worst expectations on her even though her behavior did not warrant them. In time he lost his job because he was unwilling to accept change in his industry.

Change threatens all of us. We are creatures of habit—our patterns become comfortable. What we do not know or have not experienced is therefore unknown. The fear of the unknown is an extremely strong motivator. If "boss" has always been applied to a man, it will acquire adjustment to accept a woman in that position. The more secure a man is, the easier his adjustment will be. A man who needs nurturing will be pleased to be "protected" and guided by a female. A man who has secretly been dependent on women for emotional strength will resist public subordination to a woman more than the emotionally secure man. As long as any man and woman do not lock themselves into this "parent-child" relationship, it will not be harmful to either of them to experiment with and adjust to new kinds of relationships in the working world.

Since so many men have assumed the "protective father" stance toward women with whom they have worked, they will fear the power of a new "parent" role for women. If a man fears the "child" within him, he will fear any relationship which puts him in contact with those feelings. If he is familiar with his own feelings, he will make adjustments more easily. All the responsibility for the uneasy transitions in this brave new world cannot be accepted by men. Women are stumbling through the infancy of these changes too. As both men and women deal with each other rationally their fears will diminish. Humanness is not limited to either of the sexes but crosses over our "role lines." Functions beyond physical limitations cannot be declared sexual. As men and women learn to accept minimal limits in their functioning, their "comfort zones" will broaden.

If you happen to be a man now working for a woman or possibly anticipating those circumstances in the future, let me suggest some guidelines for working out your new relationship.

First, see this woman in your life as you would a man! Yes, that's right! I am assuming that you might see him on the basis of his performance, not his clothing, his emotions, or the color of his hair. You might even try to find some way to identify with him! Give her that chance too.

Second, see her abilities and performance before you see her sexuality. Look at how she functions as a supervisor, an administrator, or a negotiator. Look at what she does and not at what she is. An amazing change might take place—you might like who she is in spite of yourself!

Finally, I borrow a word from the greatest of teachers: treat her as you would like to be treated. He said, "Do unto others as you would have them do to you." And he didn't exclude women from that statement.

In a far more general but penetrating comment a woman said:

> Really splendid men have an acceptance of themselves and a generosity of mind and spirit that makes them easier on themselves and easier on those around them, and sometimes they are strong and certain and sometimes they are not so sure, but they don't worry about their inconsistencies and allow women theirs as well. The best men can play all the parts, child and father, loved and lover, and play them all in every encounter. There are men who look after and men who need caring for, but one rarely finds them both in one. A man who is paternal but not patronizing, childlike but not childish, is extra special and usually ends up owning the world (Merle Shane, *Some Men Are More Perfect Than Others*).

It takes more effort to lead the way in the transitional experiences of life than to follow where others have led. We call those who go first pioneers. The man who accepts changes in the working world and his relationships to women there may not be alone in the future. There is, however, a certain satisfaction in having led the way. Surely there is enough pioneer spirit left in us that we will conquer the brave new world rather than be satisfied with retreating to past norms.

10

I MISS HER!

Life is like an onion:
you peel off one layer at a time,
and sometimes you weep.

—Carl Sandburg

"Excuse me," he said, and I heard the sound of throat-clearing and nose-blowing on the phone. His pain and tears were obvious. I sought to let him know that I could feel his pain, but I could not promise him that his wife would try again to work on his marriage. Only a year-and-a-half earlier the scene had been so different. She had been crying and feeling desperate; he had been resolute about his decision to leave her. On that day I had felt her deep sense of rejection and loss. There was another woman in his life. The promise of the relationship with her looked so inviting that he was not only ready but anxious to leave behind their six-plus years of marriage. He did.

She had reluctantly signed the divorce papers and slowly adjusted to the change in her life. I had listened to his story over the phone that day. After marrying the other woman and then seeing a psychiatrist for six months, he began trying to drown his depression in alcohol. Then a friend at work invited him to church, and there he experienced a meaningful conversion. Now he wanted to leave his second wife and come back home—surely that would make things all right!

Like many others, he felt that the way to "right" his life was the way "back." Too often we mistake return for retribution. Sometimes we cannot go back to places where we were in our lives and begin again.

Divorce Is Tough for Men, Too!

The world of the formerly married often resembles a maze-like existence. Much activity but little progress seems to mark the road the divorced man travels. Just when he believes that he has his directions lined up, he may discover a new derailment. Habits take time to establish and time to change. If a man has lived with a woman in marriage for several years, he has "balanced" and justified himself, and he has used his wife for complementarity in numerous subtle ways. Many of these he could not delineate if his life depended on it. But he discovers them slowly but surely in separation and divorce.

If he remains in "their" house, he sees "her" chair. He may be the only person at the table when he eats. There are empty drawers and there is excess closet space.

Normally when dealing with grief, there is a symbolic "end" when the memorial service is concluded and the body of the loved one is put into the earth. But at the end of a marriage there is no such symbol. For numerous reasons the grief is more difficult to handle. The divorcee deals with a sense of isolation and the problem of loneliness.

Reactions Vary

Every marriage counselor has had the experience of having someone come to him who has just been divorced and is asking for help in adjusting to a new life-style. The ways they come can be very different. Some come with a question—what is there worth living for? This usually reflects depression and despair. Another is the angry-bitter approach, in which a person lashes out at his mate—why won't she tell me the truth? Or why won't she be honest enough to say there is another man in her life now? In the hurt and fear is an almost universal need which is reflected in the life of the divorcee: he is lonely. He must face a new dimension in this world in which he is isolated from some of the known patterns of his previous living relationship. Even if the divorced man intellectually knows that he is headed for a brighter future than the relationship which he just ended, he is still faced with a predictable period of adjustment to his sense of loneliness and isolation.

Adjustment Problems

There are some basic factors which must be considered in order to help the individual understand what is happening to him. First, there is a definite physical loneliness and isolation. Unless the marriage has been extremely short or terribly hostile, a person has learned through the period of his marriage to be aware of the physical presence of another person in his life. He now sleeps in an empty bed. Even if he is carrying on a sexual relationship with another person, he is not physically with that person most of the time and so he has the phenomenon of the solitary bedroom. He may also be facing for the first time that empty seat at the table, a seat which has been filled by a mate over some period of years. There are certain parts of the house or the apartment that will remind him of the presence of that person and now of the absence of that person. This is true not only for the divorcee but also for the widow or widower who has lost a loved one. Something within him fights back to say "No, it isn't true—she is going to come home tonight or she will be back in that familiar spot." But there are grim physical reminders around every divorcee that a permanent change has rooted out the presence of someone to whom he has become accustomed. More important than the physical changes is the psychological impact of loneliness. If he has experienced hostility and bitterness during the conflicts of the final years of the marriage, there is nevertheless a missing part of the system of that marriage. The anticipation of joy where there was sadness or hope where there was once despair will not remove the lonely interval between the phase just ended and the phase not yet fully operational in his life. He is tempted to go back to the known pain of the situation he had in exchange for this unknown fear of what the future holds for him.

Three Universal Needs

In his book *Firo*, William Schutz postulates that there are three universal, interpersonal needs. He calls these inclusion, control, and affection. By *inclusion* he means that kind of behavior which will produce a sense of alliance and identification or which will establish and maintain a satisfactory relationship with people. By *control* he means that kind of behavior which is necessary to place oneself in an advantageous position in a relationship with respect to control and power in that relationship. By *affection* he means that kind of behavior which helps one establish and maintain satisfactory relationships with others with respect to love and affection.

The divorcee is faced immediately with the opposite of these needs: exclusion, the absence of control and power in a previously significant relationship, and no maintenance of a satisfactory relationship which will give love and affection. Isolation tends to raise questions in his mind about his own sense of judgment and values. He asks, "Did I make the right decision? Am I certain that this is what I wanted to do?" He can no longer engage in behavior that will include him in "her" life. He has no one to control other than perhaps his children. He is painfully aware of his need for and lack of affection. He finds the source for change within himself.

Self-Discovery Brings Hope

The advice which Thelonius gave his son in Shakespeare's play—"To thine own self be true, and it must follow as night follows day, thou canst not then be false to any man"—applies to the divorcee. The way out of personal dilemma is to discover someone else with whom one can share oneself, whether that person be professional or nonprofessional. It helps break the loneliness barrier when he can share himself with another person. In doing this he discovers what Sidney Jourard has called his "transparent self." He learns that in opening himself to another person, he discovers his own truth and he can no longer deceive another person or himself.

Loneliness is the basic lot of the initial phase of divorce; it is fraught with much anxiety and fear. A basic fear of isolation is whether or not we are genuinely acceptable to other people. Daniel Webster said that one of the reasons people can't stand being alone is that they don't like their own company. When we are alone, we often question whether or not we please other people. The answers are not always pleasant. If the divorcee feels rejected in the court action or in the social circumstances where he has lived, he may feel even more unacceptable than he might ordinarily feel.

Please Like Me

He may engage in something which we call introjection. To be acceptable he may emulate the feelings and emotions of other people. He is swept back and forth by all the strong people who come into his life; he simply assumes their emotional stances or accepts readily their advice.

Al had a new "buddy" every month after his divorce. Each new friend was a "great guy"! Whatever that man did to make him happy with his divorced condition, Al tried. Friend number one was a bar hopper. So for a month Al was in and out of all the bars in his city on Friday and Saturday nights, trying to pick up somebody who would be a companion or perhaps a potential spouse. The next friend, in contrast, was a churchgoer! For the next month or two Al was in and out of the local congregations in the community. Church suppers, choir parties, and other activities of the church became Al's bill of fare. He thought his newfound friend had the answer. It was an improvement, but Al was introjecting. By trying to find stability to face his loneliness, he became a carbon copy! Al could attach himself to a counselor, minister, or strong friend and identify like a shadow. But he soon discovered that a copy adds nothing to the original. He had to discover and learn to love himself before he found stability. From that anchor he could begin to love others.

When asked about the greatest of the commandments, Jesus might well have been addressing the divorced man when he said, "Love your neighbor as you love yourself." You cannot be pleased with others until you can find pleasure in the person within you.

You Can't Escape Yourself!

Escapism is another response to the loneliness of a divorce. Meaningful activity often results in a sense of well-being. However, activity without meaning only increases your sense of isolation.

"I don't belong with those people," Nick complained. "I'm just out of place." I had to agree. He was the only divorced person in a small congregation he visited. "Family night" suppers didn't *feed* him physically or spiritually—they simply reminded him of his aloneness. In a larger church he found other singles and divorcees as well as a sense of identification.

"Irrational" Failure

Many men feel that because they have been unable to be a good husband to one person in life, it automatically means that they will fail at all other relationships. This represents irrational thinking. A legitimate failure in a marriage on one occasion doesn't include automatic disaster in another attempt. Negative experiences are associated with the conclusion of a marriage. The charges and countercharges thrown back and forth by spouses leave one feeling somehow that the accusations must be true. Of course this is inaccurate.

This irrationality is strong. The man who accepts his mistakes and learns how to forgive himself for the past becomes free. The self-imposed "future failure" becomes a relationally handicapped person, unable to face new ventures in living.

Unfounded Guilt

For some partners the end of a marriage brings not only grief but also relief. Harry seemed depressed when he sat down in my office. He said he was feeling some guilt because he didn't miss his wife even though he should! He had read books on divorce and was making a pretty good adjustment. He reminded me of the fellow who, when served his breakfast by the waitress, asked her to scowl at him so he would feel at home! To be relieved from the pressure and conflict that he had lived with for the last nine years *seemed* good because it *was* good! But Harry had a strong "parent" within him that wanted to keep intact the old patterns of behavior induced by guilt.

Anxiety

Ben seemed tired and overworked with his "new" family life, but his self-concept had grown. When his wife first left him and the children to become a "runaway wife," he experienced great anger. But as he accepted his circumstances he filled in the losses with new depth in relating to his children. The "fear of losing her" had now become a reality, and he discovered he could cope with it. Fear is easier to deal with than anxiety. Anxiety is undifferentiated—a pervading sense of apprehension, an unspecified attack on the psyche. Fear is specific, and therefore I can mobilize my resources to meet it. The anxiety that he may fail at a marriage—sometimes described as the "fear of failure"—becomes a reality for the divorced man. Then he frees some of his resources to face the adjustment. He faces another ocean without a chart, but at least he sailed in the seas before and will hopefully have learned from some of these previous errors.

Look At Your Options!

Take charge of your life! You may choose a life-style for singles now—pursue that! Choose to seek another marriage! Choose a period of life in which to simply reserve judgment about the question of marriage. Take time to gain self-understanding, perhaps working with a professional. Read. Develop.

An interesting phenomenon of divorce is how quickly one seems to want to marry again. Marriage is like a beseiged city—those inside want out and those outside want in again! If you are divorced, use the time to choose carefully what you want. You may never again be as free to pursue your individual interests. To do so does not mean choosing single life forever. Try out some options—they may be to your much-unexpected satisfaction. If you marry again, your interim experiences that contribute to your happiness will become investments that pay dividends in your new relationship!

Begin Now!

You must be the prime mover in your own experience! If your wife initiated things social, invite some friends out or in for an evening! Decisions may become more difficult for you, but begin to take charge of your own life. Someone has shared responsibilities with you in the past; now she does not.

There will never be a better day to begin *your* new life than today. It is the first day of your future—the rest of your life.

11

BEYOND THE LIMITS!

*Peace is not needing to know
what's going to happen next!*

Being a man in a woman's world is not at all bad. I began this book describing a man's first relationship with a woman—from her womb. Some men never get untracked from this protective or *material* view of women. If a man wants to be "mothered" all his life, all he really has to do is play helpless. He can act like a child whether he looks like a child or not. And usually some woman will step in to take care of him. There are enough maternal women in our world so that almost every man can survive, even if he has to change "mothers" a few times in his life experience. Women provide protection for men in the world in the early years of life, but unless a man moves outside the world of protection in relationship to a woman he is only part-man. He is still a child-man, afraid to enter into the full world of reality.

Beyond Mother

Fred was a child-man when I met him. He held a position of authority and boasted of his awareness of himself. In each crisis of life, however, he sought for a woman to protect him. When the crisis passed, and he no longer needed to lean on her, he discarded her by attacking her virtue, faithfulness, or demands on him. He was a woman-hater! "They're all alike," he said. "If they gain control, they will take you to the cleaners."

Fred taught me that men who constantly fight for control of women fear their own dependence on women. Fred could not be held responsible for his mother's influence on him, but he seemed to be controlled by it. She had regularly invited him to "return to the womb" by coming home when a crisis arose in his life. When he felt "safe," the same uneasy independence led him out into the world to "free himself." Each time he married he was searching emotionally for mother. Each marriage failed because he found her! When he began to see how he was responding to his mother's influence he finally accepted responsibility for himself and he began to become a man. I hope the process is still going on.

"Momism" is a crippling disease. A man who has it needs to cut the umbilical cord before it strangles him. If your "woman's world" is predominantly a safe haven, it's time to grow up!

Beyond Playmate

Another segment of our relationship to women comes when we reach the *adult-adult* level. Here there is a new "give-and-take" experience of equality that causes some men to stumble. Some men get fixated into the playboy category and see women only as sexual objects for the satisfaction of their physical urges or as the satisfier of such emotional needs as prowess and conquest. If a man gets hung up at this point, then he never really knows the joy of sharing with a woman. He certainly cannot make a commitment to her, and his real relationships in life will be those he has with *men* to whom he can talk about his conquests and not with the women on whom he may indulge his ego or perpetrate his "masculinity." This is a blatant form of homosexuality at the emotional level. Any man who becomes fixated at this level of functioning needs to reexamine for himself what the meaning of this behavior is.

Ed was a "super jock." He had lettered in four sports ten years ago, but he still exercised regularly and was an avid tennis and golf player. If he could have shared this with his wife and children, he might have had some great family experiences. He was shattered by his wife's affair with an "inferior" man when he came to see me.

As we dug into Ed together, he made some interesting discoveries! He found, as he examined his behavior, that he entered his wife's world only as a sexual performer. He learned also that his self-esteem was built on competition with men and their admiration for his athletic and business prowess.

In a group experience he found that women could respond to his feelings. He translated that insight into new behavior with his wife. Before long he and his wife were struggling to live in an adult world instead of a protracted teenage syndrome.

Beyond Chauvinism

The third level of functioning in relationship to women is when a man enters into the *protective* role. When he has a little girl of his own, he plays the role of father. There is a special kind of response in the heart of a man to his own daughter. Some men, however, treat all women as though they were little girls. They don't have to enter into the world of physical fatherhood in order to experience these kinds of relationships.

Much "chauvinism" is perpetrated on women by men functioning in this way. Of course, it is enhanced by the women who enjoy being protected.

George was a real Southern gentleman. He called most women "honey," and his wife seemed to like his style. When I met him, he was in his third affair with a "baby doll" secretary. Because he saw himself as the great father figure he had become vulnerable. As "father," he should be able to meet any need his "girl" had. If she was not being loved by her husband, he should make sure she felt and experienced love. If she needed money, he should give it. The story could go on, ad nauseum. George was prey to his own "god" complex. He had to prove himself "the all-sufficient Daddy." He really made a mess of his life, and in the long run he would not face change.

The protective male also sets himself up to get steamrolled by the rebellious liberationist! She will nail his hide to the cross, and he will protest his innocence—a game many women and men are playing today.

Flexibility Wins

One of the great actors of physical fatherhood is in changing dimensions. Fathers are rightfully dependable for their own daughters and give them a special security in which to begin to mature. As a daughter matures she depends less on her father and more on herself. The more rebellious she is, the more she radiates her discomfort in the shift from dependence to independence. Conversely, the more protective he is the more he reflects his insecurity with the changing role of his daughter. A man with a poor transition experience with his own mother is likely to experience problems with all women, particularly his wife and daughter.

Other Women in Your Life

Every man has decisions to make about how he is going to relate to other women in his life—not his mother, his wife, or his daughter, but the *other* part of that female world out there. In this arena of experiencing women, a man will have to relate to other women at the emotional, physical, and spiritual levels of his life.

Bankers use five words that start with the letter "c" to evaluate loans—character, capacity, capital, collateral, and condition. It dawned on me recently that these factors determine the way we relate to women.

A man's *character* defines the integrity of his relationships with women. A woman cannot trust a man who does not trust himself. If he asks her in covert or open ways to take responsibility for their relationship, he will manipulate her for his own gain. He has poor male-female relationship character.

A man's *capacity* defines the limits of his relations to women. If he is able to perceive only the physical world, he will relate to women only as bodies. If he perceives the emotional level, he relates to women as interesting and exciting persons from whom he can learn. If he touches the spiritual level, the depth core of life, he will trust and be trusted by women.

A man who knows his own capacity will negotiate openly with all the women in his life about their expectations of him and his of them. One of the marks of mature capacity is the ability to affirm a woman without being manipulatively seductive. Women trust a man like that; he feels comfortable with women.

A man's *capital* determines the depth of his relationships. In business the capital is a major determinant of the strength of the corporation. So it is in man-woman relationships. A man who knows little of himself has less to offer a woman than a man who is familiar with his body, his personality, and his spirit. Persons who complain of "outgrowing" their spouses have not really been surprised. A person's growth is dependent on the real investment of himself which he makes. The more he discloses to others, the more he knows himself. A man who is a poor communicator of himself—verbally and/or nonverbally—is a bad risk in a marriage. He has already said that his investment, or commitment, to the relationship is shallow, and where his *capital*—his personhood—is committed, his performance will follow. A committed man is going to show his beloved how he feels in his behavior. Jesus put it, "Where a man's riches are, there is his heart too."

A man's *collateral* determines his style of relating to women. He offers "real equity" in return for what he expects. What Jackson and Lederer describe as "the quid pro quo" of a relationship is the "give to get" balance. How a man relates to his wife, his daughter, his mother, or any other woman is determined by the balance he sees in what he is asked to give as compared to what he gets from their relationship. A father who invests more energy, time, and money in his daughter than in his wife is "broadcasting" his feelings about what he is getting from the two relationships.

Finally, a man's *condition* is the measure of his present awareness of how he relates to others. The "condition" of the economy may devalue certain investments and add value to the posture of others. A man who is sensitive to his daily behavior and the corresponding responses he gets is on top of his relationships. As he gets out of touch with where he is in relation to others, he is in need of an update of his emotional condition.

To summarize these parallels, a man's relationship to all the women in his life is based on a broad examination of his internal feelings, his past performances, his present commitments, the way he negotiates, and his ability to assess his immediate reactions.

A man is not who he is on the basis of delegated authority from a woman or imagined responsibility for a woman. Instead, he is a maturing man as he risks knowing himself, as he trusts himself in relation to others, and as he willingly grants others the same freedom to be what he wants for himself.

Being *that* man, he will fill any woman's world with an unending challenge and an unsurpassed reward.

PART 3

FINDING
FATHERING
FULFILLING

*Reverence for God
gives a man deep strength;
his children have a place
of refuge and security.*

—Proverbs 14:26, *The Living Bible*

12

THE BALANCING ACT
—TIME

*Some men see things
the way they are and ask, why?
I see things the way they could be
and ask, why not?"*

—George Bernard Shaw

Have you experienced a weekend when you planned to spend some time with your children only to discover that they have already made plans with their friends and have obtained permission from their mother to carry out those plans? Have you planned a vacation to surprise the whole family and then been told, much to your disappointment, that nobody else thinks it's a good idea? Then you have begun to recognize that "father sometimes knows last."

One problem in a man's world is the demand on his time. There are multiple demands for his time—from his job, his community, and his family. In the family, the wife rightly demands the first commitment.

The Marital Relationship

One of the most interesting studies that I have ever read indicated that children in therapy made progress when those children began to perceive that the relationship between father and mother was closer than the relationship between either of the parents and the children. Mom and Dad ought to have the strongest commitment to each other, and the children ought to be aware of that in an emotionally healthy home.

That is a tough act to bring off! So often the mother is forced by the pressure of time to be closer to the children and their decisions than the father is allowed to be, particularly if he travels. His profession may demand long hours away from home, which is perhaps worse than the strain of travel itself.

Coping with any problem is for me a matter of priorities: I believe that the greatest gift a father gives his children is to love their mother. Other things follow in the course of parental priorities!

The Father's Responsibility

After a man becomes a father, he no longer has the luxury of philosophizing about child-rearing. Before my children were born, I could easily *authoritatively* quote principles of parenthood. After experiencing parenthood for a few years I found I had *suggestions* to make about how to deal with children. The older my children get the more I seem simply to be *sharing* with other parents the ways I cope with that responsibility.

It is, of course, a man's own loss when he cannot spend time with his children. One of the things that I discover in dealing with fathers is that there is a great deal of *guilt* about the failure to spend time with children. As impudent as it may sound, I think dads ought to stop feeling guilty about not meeting the expectations of their wives or their children. A man must make his own decision about how much time he is going to spend with his children, and that will vary from man to man. He must evaluate how well he functions with children. Some men, like some women, will relate to their children better at certain ages than at other ages. Every father needs to know his own strength well enough to be able to determine what he will do at this point.

Jack's Story

I can illustrate this with Jack. At our first meeting he seemed a bit defensive, although by all appearances he was a competent professional. He said he had a family problem, and he wasn't kidding! He had a hysterical wife and three rebellious and undisciplined children. His wife cried uncontrollably and bitterly as she accused him of failing her and their children.

One of my "North Stars" in the seas of counseling came to mind as I met with Jack. Whatever a man says or does makes some kind of sense to *him*, even if it sounds crazy to me! I asked Jack to spend some time letting me get to know *him* before working with his family. He agreed. As I discovered Jack, he discovered himself.

Jack had a passive, but controlling father and a dominant mother. His model taught him that men are quiet and avoid open conflicts. In the academic pursuit, Jack excelled and enjoyed the open approval of professors. He knew that when people praised him, it made him feel good. He also learned that when he handled conflicts openly in his professional world it resulted in satisfactory resolution.

But Jack had the problem of not being able to *translate* what he learned professionally into *personal behavior*. When he came home, he repeated the learned patterns of his father's example. He became quiet, performing well but escaping into himself by drinking, and he had little communication with his wife or children.

As Jack began to see that his professional successes resulted from some good qualities in himself, he accepted the possibilities of being more successful in his home life. We worked on self-assertion. He learned to like himself.

Before too long Jack's strength and courage began to show at home. He drank less and didn't miss it. He talked to his wife and children about his feelings, and he discovered that they were interested in him. The more he shared with his wife, the less frantic she appeared to him. He risked making some firm demands on the children, even when they verbally rebelled at his new strength. But they responded to his leadership!

Laws of Parental Power

Jack illustrates the three laws of parental power. First, *I can only influence my children when I believe in who I am as a person.* I cannot love another person if I do not love myself. If that has a New Testament ring to it, you'll find that Jesus and Paul said it before me. They just used different words.

The second principle for parents is that *I can only expect my children to believe in the behavior I model for them.* As Jack saw what his father had modeled, he clearly chose to attempt another course with his own children. It began to work. It is true that "Children Learn What They Live."

If a child lives with criticism, he learns to condemn.

If a child lives with hostility, he learns to fight.

If a child lives with shame, he learns to feel guilty.

If a child lives with tolerance, he learns to be patient.

If a child lives with encouragement, he learns confidence.

If a child lives with fairness, he learns justice.

If a child lives with security, he learns to have faith.

If a child lives with approval, he learns to like himself.

If a child lives with acceptance and friendship, he learns

to find love in the world.

—Dorothy Law Nolte

The third principle for parents is that *I will only know my children as I risk sharing myself with them.* As Jack opened up, both in his strengths and in his weaknesses, to his wife and children, they became more responsive to him as a person. He was more than a "role"—he was a whole being with his family. It is interesting to note that I never saw Jack's children professionally. They didn't need a psychologist—they needed a father. In time Jack helped himself and helped his family through their crisis.

13

FATHERS:
MADE IN CRISIS

Hope is not a dream,
but a way of making dreams
become reality!

Being a father is a balance between the joys and the frustrations of life. Nobody gets only joy or only frustration—fortunately! We wouldn't appreciate the joy without the frustration, and we couldn't tolerate the problems without moments of reward.

Tragedy Teaches

Occasionally I feel that fathers should have a label sewed onto their backbones which reads "Made in Crisis." At least for me, crisis in a hospital has been a crucible for blending my helpless and hopeful feelings as a father.

It was a tragic scene. My son was lying on the ground with a mangled, bleeding foot. Frenzied but genuinely concerned neighbors gathered like flies, as they always do at an accident. The father of the boy riding the lawn mower tried to explain how it happened, but the explanation made little sense. Fortunately the ambulance arrived only seconds after I did.

The siren blared against the oncoming traffic as we raced the few blocks to Northside Hospital. I held onto my thirteen-year-old son's left leg, bracing his foot with my other arm. I knew the leg was broken but all the attention was on the foot which had been almost severed by the riding lawn mower.

Then followed the almost bizarre experience of a hospital emergency room, surgical preparation, the seemingly eternal waiting during operations, and the first hospital stay of ten days to begin the process of recovery.

I usually do pretty well in crisis. I see a good deal of it in my work as a marriage and family counselor. Twenty years as a clergyman and office practitioner has given me many insights.

Parental Perspectives

This personal experience gave me new perspectives—parental ones! When your child is hospitalized from an accident, you face unusual feelings. You feel *angry* that this happened to your child, and anger looks for a scapegoat. Why did the boy on the mower lose control? Shouldn't the design of riding mowers be changed to prevent these kinds of accidents? I knew it would not help to blame others.

Blaming yourself won't help either. Why didn't you warn him? If you had been at the neighbor's house, perhaps the accident could have been avoided. Neurotic guilt crowds your mind. I've learned that neurotic guilt is that guilt about which I can do nothing. Real guilt can be changed by some direct action, such as an apology, restitution, confession, etc.

Parents of hospitalized children are faced with their own *helplessness*. It's particularly hard on a daddy whose son thinks he can do anything! You can't make the pain go away. You can't provide medical services. It's tough to feel helpless and dependent on others. Dependency touches the greatest core of inadequacy in any of us. I was no exception.

Impatience also places a tough demand on the parent of the hospitalized child. Some nurses, doctors, and other auxiliary staff in a hospital seem inexcusably slow. Few are deliberately avoiding doing something for your child, but one's paranoid tendencies can get badly overworked in that situation.

Fatigue sets in before long and becomes a contribution to parental malfunction. It becomes easier to snap at a nurse, your spouse, or one of your other children when you're overly tired.

The question of "medical diagnosis" can be almost amusing! The doctor is so careful he usually says little; the frustration often leads the parents to hypothesize, generalize, and elaborate on their own.

Lessons Learned

I learned two important things about myself as a parent while my son was hospitalized.

First, I wasn't a total failure as a parent. Here was my "child" of thirteen years functioning at what seemed to be superhuman levels. He seemed like a Trojan—so strong—"my little man." Whatever sense of his own personhood had been developing, it solidified, and he became an adult in many ways. It warmed my "parent" heart to see it happen.

Second, no matter how helpless I felt, my child still needed his father. "Dad, move my leg, please." "Let Dad do it" spoken to a nurse became like sweet music to the "helpless" father. It's nice to be needed! Most of all, I saw his eyes looking for reassurance. There was no need to try to lie and say the pain was gone and "everything would be fine soon," for he knew this wasn't true. But I could say honestly I would be there. There were many nights when the bed at home would have given more rest, but the cot in his room gave more satisfaction.

Early one morning, as I watched the sun rise and saw jets circling for Hartsfield International Airport, I looked at Jimmy in a peaceful sleep. I thought of the words of the Psalmist—"I will fear no evil, for *Thou* art with me." My child slept because he was aware *I* was present. When a crisis in the family comes, there is so much strength in knowing that father is there. And every man finds his heavenly Father present in crisis.

Communicate—Avoid the Crises!

If a father fails to know, it may be the result of having insulated himself from his wife and children. Learning to communicate what your own feelings are to your spouse and children gives a man great freedom in his family. I don't promise it will be easy to do this. It may take several efforts and some patience when you feel rebuffed. But begin—any way you can!

One of the crucial points for me in dealing with the young woman in my life, my daughter, is keeping lines of communication open. She faces peer pressure, and I face time pressure. That makes it awfully difficult for us to get together. I try to make sure that I listen well enough when we are together to keep the lines of communication open between us. I discovered that one of the ways she keeps those lines open with her friends is by writing notes and letters. So I learned a lesson from my daughter! I wrote her this letter on her thirteenth birthday:

Dear Joy,

When special occasions arise in a person's life, it seems to me that a little time for reflection is in order. Your special occasion for now is a thirteenth birthday.

Thirteen years ago I stood in the hospital in Pomona, California, and breathed a prayer of thanksgiving at your birth. For a few hours the doctors had worried about the complications that caused you to be born by the Caesarean section method. Our *joy* at your birth so near the celebration of Jesus' birth made picking your name an easy assignment. Of course, the "Marie" is from your mother's name. Next to her, you are my special girl.

As you grew up, you were at times a joy—sometimes you were just very funny! You almost always had a cheery smile for everyone. That's a quality I hope you'll never lose. There's a glow about people who are sure of themselves that relaxes and refreshes those around them.

One of the happiest days of my life was the night in your bedroom in Athens when I listened as you asked Christ to be Lord of your life. And I was extremely proud to be able to baptize you that following Sunday night. There are some joys that fathers who are not ministers cannot share with their daughters.

Thirteen is a very special age. The teen years are fantastic and very problematic. You know how many parents come to me to talk about how to get along with their children. You are on the road to physical adulthood and emotional maturity.

At this point in your life, I want to ask you to help your mother and me to be the best parents we can be to you as a teenager. One of the things we will need is to have you talk to us about your feelings. Information questions are all right too, but talk to us about the things you want to share or the things about which you are not sure. We may not know answers to all problems, but we can listen because we love you. Those two things are very important in life—to be listened to and to be loved! We also need to have you listen to us at times, and we will always need your love.

I could get carried away with this letter, but I'll stop with a pledge to you. With your help, I'll try to be the best father I can be during your teen years. The world isn't what it was when I was your age; I'll try not to set back the clock! I love you very much. I want you to be as proud of me as your father as I am that you're my daughter.

Happy Birthday!
Daddy

Weighed or Wanting?

Written communication or oral communication—both are necessary. Most of us who are breadwinners in the family are going to have to fight for time to spend with our children and for opportunities not to miss out on some precious moments in their lives. It will mean making critical decisions when the pressures they put on us seem not to be as great as the pressures of our vocational world. Weigh those decisions carefully. Someday it may be too late to have a second chance with your child.

14

IS GOD A FATHER?

*God's most insistent call to us
will always seem a sort of silence,
since His language
isn't what we expect.*

—Evely

Textbooks about psychological development say it is difficult for a person to appreciate what the role of a good father is if he has had no model. Of course, if he had a "bad" father, then it would be very difficult for him to think of God as a "good" father. The theological world is full of references to God as Father. I sat down the other day and tried to say what having God as a Father means to me.

God's Fatherhood

One of the first things I discovered is that having God as my Father means *closeness*. As a boy when I had a paper route, I remember my dad getting up early on rainy Sunday mornings to go with me in the car and help me deliver the unusually large papers that we had on Sunday. I always appreciated that, and I felt close to my dad at those times when we were working together. I remember feeling close when we went hunting together or we did some of the other father-son activities, although these were somewhat infrequent between us.

As I think about God, the overriding quality I want to maintain in my relationship to Him is this quality of closeness. Fatherhood is a kind of automatic door to intimacy. There are some things a father has access to in the lives of his children that no one else has. In the same way there are some things that a child has access to in the life of his father that no one else does. God's "fatherhood" only becomes a reality when we allow Him to be close to us and to share our lives.

Integrity

A second important term describing man's relationship to God is *integrity*. For me the hierarchy of personal integrity is summed up in three questions:

Is what I'm about to do in keeping with my character and personhood?

Is what I'm about to do in keeping with commitments that I have made to the "intimate" members of my world (my wife, my family, etc.)?

Is what I'm about to do going to serve as an example to anyone else who may view that action?

God as Father provides me with a base of integrity. God made me to be a man with certain potential, ability, and capacity that I want to fulfill.

Sin is not so much an act against God, but a failure to live out God's gifts in one's experience. My "sin" against my father would be to fail to respond to the things he has given me as his child. So in my relationship to God, sin is failing to live out my potential as a person. For me that potential is far more freeing than it is limiting. God's "fatherhood" is not a set of rules against which I measure the acceptability of my life before Him, but is instead an encouragement to be all that I can be as His son.

Loneliness

A third thing that God's fatherhood means to me is in the area of *loneliness*. Because I believe that not only is there an existent God, but a personal being whom I can call Father, I can never be alone in the universe.

I remember reading for the first time those words from Robert Burns' poem about home: "Home's a place when you have to go there they have to take you in." As long as a person has a home (or family) he always has a place to go when he needs it. As long as a man has a father, there is someplace he can turn to. As long as God exists, I as a man do not have to be lonely. I am persuaded that being a child of God is not the result of being bribed by a sense of needing God's approval or by the promise of material goods if I act the way I ought to so that I'll receive God's blessings. It is not the result of being threatened with the punishment of hell or some other inscrutable judgment. It is instead the result of a kind of persuasion that grows out of my loneliness.

I am aware that there are two kinds of fears that drive a man. The first is the fear that *someone will know him as he really is*. Because of this fear he wears a "mask" to keep other people away from him. He hides and pretends and deceives. But there is a far greater fear in all of us—the fear that *no one will ever know us*. If no one ever knows me, my loneliness remains intact and is the most powerful force in my experience. So one of the goals of life is to let someone enter into the world, the secret world, within us and know us as we are. The "new birth" that is spoken of in the New Testament is the moment when I allow God to permeate the innermost part of my being. At that moment I open myself up to the loss of loneliness and the experience of having a friend who is my Father.

Discovering Wholeness

Outside my own family I derive the most personal satisfaction from my work. I feel very fortunate to "get into" many people's lives. One of the ways this occurs is in my personal growth groups.

These experiences are limited to eight adult men and women who meet together for 25 hours over a ten-week period. One of the major aspects of this experience is the opportunity to disclose oneself to others and in the process come to know oneself better.

There is a constant reaffirmation in this process as I see men and women feeling more confident about themselves as they learn to relate to each other honestly. This has become a "religious" experience for many group members. They have not only become aware of their own feelings and the feelings of others, but have become aware of the presence of God in the group.

While there is no specific theological instruction in these groups, it has never surprised me that people experience God here. Where wholeness occurs, God is present, even if not acknowledged. For me, that provides significant data about God as Father.

As I invest myself in another person by disclosing who I am, a new dimension of my value and worth is inherently given to him. As he reveals himself to me, he decreases my loneliness by bridging the distance between us.

I like one of Keith Miller's thoughts: "If you can describe a problem clearly enough and I have the same problem, suddenly I am no longer alone with my problems, and somehow you have become God to me."

I read a clear account in Biblical history of God's sharing Himself with me. As I have responded, I have discovered who my Father really is. That discovery has freed me to find hope in all the dimensions of my relationships to other men and women—hope about being a man in today's world.

I am not everything I have described in this book at all times, but I have experienced the reality of every idea here. I know of no greater hope than to be more of a man today than I was yesterday and less than I will be tomorrow. As Robert Browning said, "A man's reach should always exceed his grasp."